BILLY GRAHAM
Evangelistic Association
Always Good News.

Dear Friend,

I am pleased to send you this special version of *Hope for Each Day: Words of Wisdom and Faith* by my father, Billy Graham, with specific information and prayer requests related to the *My Hope with Billy Graham* project.

In this devotional, my father presents a Scripture for each day of the year and then shares his thoughts on that selection, with practical application of each verse to our everyday lives. I trust that you will be encouraged and strengthened as you read these passages, and "*I pray that the eyes of your heart may be enlightened, so that you will know what is the hope of His calling, what are the riches of the glory of His inheritance*" (Ephesians 1:18, NASB).

For more than 60 years, the Billy Graham Evangelistic Association has worked to take the Good News of Jesus Christ throughout the world by every effective means available, and I'm excited about what God will do in the years ahead.

We would appreciate knowing how our ministry has touched your life. May God richly bless you.

Sincerely,

Franklin Graham
President

If you would like to know more about our ministry, please contact us:

IN THE U.S.:
Billy Graham Evangelistic Association
1 Billy Graham Parkway
Charlotte, NC 28201-0001
BillyGraham.org
info@bgea.org
Toll-free: 1-877-247-2426

IN CANADA:
Billy Graham Evangelistic
  Association of Canada
20 Hopewell Way NE
Calgary, AB T3J 5H5
BillyGraham.ca
Toll-free: 1-888-393-0003

W9-BJV-623

HOPE

for Each Day

Words of Wisdom and Faith

This special edition is published for the
Billy Graham Evangelistic Association
by Thomas Nelson, Inc.

COUNTRYMAN ®

A Division of Thomas Nelson Publishers

THOMAS NELSON ®
Since 1798

NASHVILLE DALLAS MEXICO CITY RIO DE JANEIRO

Unless otherwise indicated, all Scripture quotations in this book are from the New King James Version (NKJV) ©1982, Thomas Nelson, Inc., and are used by permission.

Other Scripture references are from the following sources:

The New International Version of the Bible (NIV) ©1973, 1978, 1984, 2011 by Biblica, Inc. Used by permission. All rights reserved worldwide.

The Jerusalem Bible (TJB) ©1968 by Darton, Longman & Todd, Ltd., and Doubleday & Co., Inc.

The New Testament: a New Translation, ©1964 by James Moffatt, published by Harper & Row, Inc. (MOFFATT).

The New American Standard Bible (NASB) ©1960, 1962, 1963, 1971, 1972, 1973, 1975, and 1977 by the Lockman Foundation. Used by permission.

The Revised Standard Version of the Bible (RSV) ©1946, 1952, 1971, 1973 by the Division of Christian Education of the National Council of the Churches of Christ in the USA. Used by permission.

The New Revised Standard Version (NRSV) ©1989 by the Division of Christian Education of the National Council of the Churches of Christ in the United States of America. Used by permission.

The King James Version of the Bible (KJV).

The Good News Bible: The Bible in Today's English Version (TEV) ©1976 by the American Bible Society.

The Living Bible (TLB) ©1971, Tyndale House Publishers, Inc., Wheaton, Ill., all rights reserved.

The Amplified Bible (AMP), Old Testament, ©1962, 1964 by Zondervan Publishing House, and from The Amplified New Testament, ©1958 by the Lockman Foundation (used by permission).

These meditations include edited excerpts from *Unto the Hills: A Daily Devotional*, by Billy Graham, and edited sermons from Billy Graham that were previously published in *Decision* magazine. These are used with the author's permission. Other meditations from the author have been prepared specifically for this volume.

ISBN: 978-1-4003-7518-9

A MOVEMENT TO

Transform Our Nation

WHAT'S YOUR IDEA OF THE AVERAGE AMERICAN COMMUNITY?

White picket fences, manicured lawns, and two cars in the garage?

The real America is not so picturesque, and it underscores the urgency of our work as Christians. If you live in the typical community—with 100 average neighbors—here's the reality:

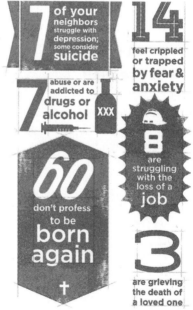

7 of your neighbors struggle with depression; some consider **suicide**

14 feel crippled or trapped by **fear & anxiety**

7 abuse or are addicted to **drugs or alcohol** XXX

8 are struggling with the loss of a **job**

60 don't profess to be **born again** †

3 are grieving the death of a loved one

OUR NATION

NEEDS THE HOPE OF

Jesus Christ

Working together with local churches and Christians like you, the Billy Graham Evangelistic Association will hold a nationwide outreach that will culminate with a powerful message from my father in November 2013.

MY HOPE *with* BILLY GRAHAM

My Hope with Billy Graham will coincide with my father's 95th birthday and will proclaim the only hope that can change our communities and transform our nation—the Gospel of Jesus Christ. The need is urgent. Will you join us—before it's too late—to lift up "God our Savior and the Lord Jesus Christ, our hope" (1 Timothy 1:1, NKJV)?

FRANKLIN GRAHAM
President, Billy Graham Evangelistic Association

WHAT IS *MY HOPE WITH BILLY GRAHAM?*

At its heart, this outreach is friends sharing Jesus with friends. It's simple:

INVITE
Invite your friends and neighbors who don't know Jesus Christ to your home for a meal or dessert.

WATCH
Then, watch the special program featuring popular music, real-life stories, and a short message from Billy Graham.

SHARE
Next, briefly share how Jesus gave you hope and tell what He is doing in your life today.

ASK
Ask your friends if they would like to make the same decision you did to receive Jesus Christ as Lord and Savior and pray with them.

SHARING *Your Story*

Here's a three-minute plan for telling your story—
how Jesus gave you hope and what He's doing in
your life today.

 Tell what your life was like before
you received Jesus.

 Explain what caused you to
turn to God.

 Share the circumstances of how
you received Him into your life.

 Repeat the prayer you prayed
to receive Jesus Christ.

 Explain how your life has changed since Jesus
became your Lord and Savior.

Once you share your story, invite your listeners to do
what you did and receive Jesus Christ as their Lord
and Savior. Ask those who want to make a decision
to pray with you:

A SAMPLE *Prayer* YOU CAN USE

*"Dear Lord Jesus, I know I am a sinner, and I ask for
Your forgiveness. I believe You died for my sins and
rose from the dead. I turn from running my own life,
and now I ask You to run it. I invite You to come into
my heart and life. I trust and follow You as my Lord
and Savior. In Jesus' Name, amen."*

MILLIONS OF PEOPLE HAVE DONE IT. SO CAN YOU.

Many Christians are nervous about sharing their faith with others. But as we've done this outreach across the globe, people just like you remark that it was well worth the effort. Following the example of the apostle Matthew (see Matthew 9:9–10), who invited friends into his home for a meal to meet Jesus, you will get all the training you need to:

 LOOK AROUND and identify your friends, neighbors, co-workers, fellow students, and family who do not know Jesus Christ as their Savior. Write their names on the next page.

 LOOK UP and pray every day for each person you have listed.

 LOOK OUT for opportunities to build your relationship with these people.

 LOOK FORWARD to the event: Invite every person on your list, prepare your three-minute story, and pray for God's help as you invite your guests to receive Jesus into their life.

 LOOK AFTER those who give their lives to Jesus Christ and help them grow in their faith, and continue your relationship with the others.

MY *Matthew* LIST

Write on the lines below the names of your friends, neighbors, and family who need Jesus Christ and His hope. Start with two or three, and God will bring more to your mind as you pray. Pray for them every day and build a strong relationship with them. Invite them to your home in November 2013.

1 _____

2 _____

3 _____

4 _____

5 _____

6 _____

7 _____

8 _____

9 _____

10 _____

Therefore I live for today—

Certain of finding at sunrise
Guidance and strength for the way.

Power for each moment of weakness,
Hope for each moment of pain,
Comfort for every sorrow,
Sunshine and joy after rain!

—ANONYMOUS

ACKNOWLEDGMENTS

*The author gratefully acknowledges
the able assistance of all who have
participated in bringing this project to
completion, especially David Moberg,
Jack Countryman, and Terri Gibbs of the
J. Countryman Division of Thomas Nelson, Inc.,
and Dr. John N. Akers of my staff.*

PREFACE

For many years I have sought to walk with God every day. What a joy it is to wake up in the morning and know He is with me, no matter what the day has in store. What a joy it is to look back in the evening and be able to thank Him for His faithfulness and to experience His peace. What a joy it is to know that someday soon the burdens of this life will be over and I will awaken in His presence!

When I think about God's love I tend to dwell upon all the good things He has done for me. But then I must stop and realize that even when circumstances have been hard or the way unclear, God has still surrounded me with His love. God's love is just as real and just as powerful in the darkness as it is in the light. And that is why we can have hope!

Every day I turn to the Bible to give me strength and wisdom for the day and hope for the future. Its words have seen me through good times and bad—through times of happiness and grief, health and sickness, victory and disappointment. God's Word can do the same for you.

May God use these daily selections to encourage you and give you hope. May they also challenge you, both to live more fully for Christ each day and to trust His great love—no matter what comes your way.

—BILLY GRAHAM

January

*Pray that God will give you His heart
for those around you who need a
relationship with Jesus Christ.*

January 1

In Tune with the Master

*You shall surround me
with songs of deliverance.*
PSALM 32:7

Out West an old sheepherder had a violin, but it was out of tune. He had no way of tuning it, so in desperation he wrote to one of the radio stations and asked them at a certain hour on a certain day to strike the tone "A." The officials of the station decided they would accommodate the old fellow, and on that particular day the true tone of "A" was broadcast. His fiddle was thus tuned, and once more his cabin echoed with joyful music.

When we live apart from God, our lives get out of tune—out of harmony with others and with God. But if we live in tune with the Master, we, too, will find ourselves surrounded by His beautiful music.

As this new year begins, ask God to help you tune your life every day to His Word, so you can bring harmony and joy to those around you.

THE SUN STILL SHINING

*They looked . . . and behold, the glory
of the Lord appeared in the cloud.*
EXODUS 16:10

Without the clouds we wouldn't be shielded from the burning sun. Without the clouds there would be no lavish sunsets, no beneficial rain, no beautiful landscapes.

The same is true with life's clouds. When hard times come we easily get discouraged. But behind the clouds God is still present, and can even use them to water our souls with unexpected blessings. Longfellow once wrote: "Be still, sad heart, and cease repining; behind the clouds is the sun still shining."

As God's people wandered in the wilderness, He declared, "Behold, I come to you in the thick cloud" (Exod. 19:9).

Each of us experiences clouds in life—sometimes slight, but sometimes dark and frightening. Whatever clouds you face today, ask Jesus, the light of the world, to help you look behind the cloud to see His glory and His plans for you.

January 3

A SPRING FOR THE SOUL

With You is the fountain of life;
in Your light we see light.
PSALM 36:9

Sadly, many people get their happiness only from outward circumstances. As long as their lives are untroubled, they feel happy. But when illness strikes, or a relationship breaks down, or any of a thousand other unexpected troubles engulf them, then happiness flees.

Near my home is a spring that never varies its flow. Floods may rage, but its output doesn't increase. A long summer's drought may come, but it won't decrease. Its flow is steady, reliable, and unending.

Such is the peace we all yearn for—and such is the peace Jesus promises to all who trust in Him: "The water that I shall give him will become in him a fountain of water springing up into everlasting life. . . . My peace I give to you" (John 4:14; 14:27).

Have you come to that unending spring—which is Christ? Are you coming to Him each day?

January 4

The Promise Is Ours

I am with you always,
even to the end of the age.
MATTHEW 28:20

When David Livingstone returned to his native Scotland after sixteen difficult years as a missionary and explorer in Africa, his body was emaciated by the ravages of some twenty-seven fevers that had coursed through his veins during the years of his service. His left arm hung useless at his side, the result of his being mangled by a lion.

Speaking to the students at Glasgow University, he said, "Shall I tell you what sustained me during the hardship and loneliness of my exile? It was Christ's promise, 'Lo, I am with you always, even to the end of the age.'"

That promise is ours as well. No matter what trials we face, Christ never leaves us. He is with us every step of the way! Keep that promise before you today—and always.

January 5

HE IS HERE TO HELP

Who shall separate us from the love of Christ?
ROMANS 8:35

After His resurrection Jesus came to His disciples, meeting them between the garden with its empty tomb and the city with its mob still passionate with hate. He said to them, "Do not be afraid. Go and tell My brethren" (Matt. 28:10).

In the midst of a world filled with danger, hatred, and war, the words of our Lord Jesus Christ are just as relevant as when He spoke them. He still says to all who love Him, "Do not be afraid."

He comes to you in the hospital room or in the midst of a family tragedy. He comes to you in the midst of an unexpected business reversal or physical crisis. And He says, "Don't be afraid. I'm alive, and I'm here to help you. The Cross shows the depth of My love, and the Resurrection shows the depth of My power. Nothing can ever separate you from Me!"

January 6

THE GLORY OF GOD

In My Father's house are many mansions....
I go to prepare a place for you.
JOHN 14:2

There was once a little boy who was riding alone on a train, and the scenery was not too interesting. A woman sitting beside him asked, "Are you tired of the long ride?"

The boy smiled and said, "I'm a little tired, but I don't mind it much. You see, my father is going to meet me when I get there."

Sometimes we get tired of the burdens of life, but we know that Jesus Christ will meet us at the end of our life's journey—and that makes all the difference. Paul wrote, "Therefore we do not lose heart.... For the things which are seen are temporary, but the things which are not seen are eternal" (2 Cor. 4:16, 18). Knowing we will be with Christ forever far outweighs our burdens today! Keep your eyes on eternity!

January 7

A SPIRIT OF THANKFULNESS

*I have learned the secret of being
content in any and every situation....*
PHILIPPIANS 4:12, NIV

Some years ago I visited a man who was wealthy and successful, the envy of all his friends and business associates. But as we talked, he broke down in tears, confessing that he was miserable inside. Wealth had not been able to fill the empty place in his heart.

A few hours later I visited another man who lived only a few miles away. His cottage was humble, and he had almost nothing in the way of this world's possessions. Yet his face was radiant as he told me about the work he was doing for Christ and how Christ had filled his life with meaning and purpose.

I went away convinced that the second man was really the rich man. Although he had very little, he had learned to be thankful for everything God had given him. A spirit of thankfulness makes all the difference.

January 8

THE TRIUMPHS OF GRACE

I, even I, am He who blots out
your transgressions. . . .
ISAIAH 43:25

When Charles Wesley experienced the joy of divine forgiveness, he told a Moravian friend of his new sense of pardon, and added, "I suppose I had better keep silent about it."

"Oh, no, my brother," came the reply. "If you had a thousand tongues, you should go and use them all for Jesus."

Charles Wesley went home and wrote the great hymn: "O, for a thousand tongues to sing / My great Redeemer's praise, / The glories of my God and King, / The triumphs of His grace!"

To a burdened, benighted world, crushed under the weight of its own wickedness, God says, "I, even I, am He who blots out your transgressions" (Isa. 43:25). This is glorious news, and it applies to all people everywhere—including you. Have you received God's gift of forgiveness? If you have, thank Him for it—and if not, by faith invite Christ into your life today.

January 9

SET FREE FROM SIN

In Him we have redemption through His blood.
EPHESIANS 1:7

A loving mother who saved her little girl from a burning house suffered severe burns on her hands and arms. When the girl grew older, not knowing how her mother's arms had become so seared, the girl was ashamed of those scarred, gnarled hands and always insisted that her mother wear long gloves to cover up the ugliness.

But one day the daughter asked her mother how her hands had become so scarred. The mother, for the first time, told her the story of how she had saved the daughter's life with those hands. The daughter wept tears of gratitude and said, "Oh, Mother, those are beautiful hands, the most beautiful in the world. Don't ever hide them again!"

Just so, the blood of Christ may seem to be a grim, repulsive subject to those who do not realize its true significance; but to those who have been rescued from sin's chains, Christ's nail-pierced hands are beautiful beyond measure, for they tell us of His love and His willingnesss to save us regardless of the cost.

THINK ETERNITY

Seek first the kingdom of God.
MATTHEW 6:33

King George V wrote on the flyleaf of the Bible of a friend: "The secret of happiness is not to do what you like to do, but to learn to like what you have to do."

Too many people think happiness is an elusive, will-o'-the-wisp thing to be found only by constant pursuit and relentless searching. But happiness is not an end in itself; it is the byproduct of something far greater. Jesus told His disciples: "Seek first the kingdom of God and His righteousness, and all these things shall be added to you" (Matt. 6:33). The "things" He spoke of were the basic needs of life: food, drink, clothes, shelter. He told us not to make these things the chief goal of our lives, but to "seek ... the kingdom."

There, if we will take it, is the secret of happiness: "Seek first the kingdom of God ..." How do we do this? By submitting ourselves without reserve to Jesus Christ as King of our lives every day. This is the path of true happiness.

January 11

FAITH GROWS BY EXPRESSION

You are the light of the world.
MATTHEW 5:14

Tom Allan, Scotland's famous preacher, was brought to Christ while a soldier was singing, "Were you there when they crucified my Lord?" He said it was neither the song nor the voice, but the spirit in which that soldier sang—something about his manner, something about his sincerity of expression—that convicted Allan of his wicked life and turned him to the Savior.

Jesus said, "You are the light of the world.... Let your light so shine before [others], that they may see your good works, and glorify your Father in heaven" (Matt. 5:14, 16).

Our faith becomes stronger as we express it; a growing faith is a sharing faith. Pray now for those you know who need Christ, and ask God to help you be a witness to them—by the life you live and the words you speak.

January 12

ALL FOR JESUS

We are in Him who is true, in His Son Jesus Christ.
1 JOHN 5:20

In His Steps, by Charles M. Sheldon, tells of a challenge given by a pastor to his people to pledge for one year not to do anything without first asking the question: "What would Jesus do?"

This challenge was kindled when a shabby man, mourning his wife who had died in poverty, stumbled into a wealthy church and addressed the congregation. He said, "I heard some people singing at a church prayer meeting the other night: 'All for Jesus! All for Jesus! / All my being's ransomed powers; / All my thoughts and words and doings, / All my days and all my hours.' I kept wondering as I sat on the steps outside just what they meant by it. It seems to me there's an awful lot of trouble in the world that somehow wouldn't exist if all the people who sing such songs went and lived them out."

If someone posed the same question to us, what would be our response? Do we live our lives with the thought, "What would Jesus do?" Do we put it into practice every day?

January 13

GOD'S HAND OF BLESSING

*Every good gift and every
perfect gift is from above.*
JAMES 1:17

In the midst of the Lord's Prayer are these familiar words: "Give us this day our daily bread" (Matt. 6:11). They remind us that we are dependent on God for everything, and He is the giver of every blessing. "Every good gift and every perfect gift is from above, and comes down from the Father of lights" (James 1:17).

Some people say, "Why should I pray for my daily bread? I can take care of my own needs!" But listen: If it weren't for God's love and grace, you wouldn't have anything. We need to pray this prayer every day, because we need to be reminded to trust God in everything.

This prayer reminds us also of Jesus' words: "I am the bread of life. He who comes to Me shall never hunger" (John 6:35). Thank God for all His gifts—especially Christ, the greatest gift of all.

January 14

CHRIST PROVIDES THE CURE

If anyone is in Christ, he is a new creation.
2 CORINTHIANS 5:17

Wouldn't it be wonderful if we could find a medicine that would absolutely cure human nature's weaknesses and failures? Conflict, discontent, and unhappiness plague people everywhere. But suppose a cure could be found for humanity's ills. It would cause a worldwide stampede!

The most thrilling news in the world is that there is a cure! God has provided the medicine—and that "medicine" is Christ. Through Him our sins can be forgiven, and by His Holy Spirit within us our lives can be changed and renewed.

Sin, confusion, and disillusionment can be replaced by righteousness, joy, and hope. Our souls can know peace, a peace that is not dependent on outward circumstances. This cure was provided two thousand years ago by Jesus Christ's death and resurrection for us. Is He working daily in your life, changing you and making you more like Him?

January 15

LOOKING FOR LASTING JOY

May the God of hope fill you with all joy.
ROMANS 15:13

How often have you found what you were looking for in life, only to realize it didn't bring you the satisfaction you thought it would?

It is life's ultimate frustration—thinking we will find fulfillment in the things of this world. But they can never bring lasting happiness. As one bumper sticker I saw expressed it, "All I want is a little more than I have now."

We look for love, security, and happiness through our jobs, our possessions, our relationships—but if they really brought lasting joy, wouldn't we have testimonies to that effect from millions of people all over the world? Instead, we find emptiness, discontent, and hopelessness.

Try putting Christ first and watch how your life is turned around. You will discover that He alone is the source of the love, peace, and joy you have been searching for.

January 16

Enjoying God's Presence

In Your presence is fullness of joy.
PSALM 16:11

Have you ever watched a young couple communicate their love for each other without even saying a word? Maybe you have experienced it yourself. Every glance, every touch, every smile conveys love. People deeply in love find absolute bliss simply being in each other's presence.

In the same way, simply being in the presence of God brings us great joy. It happens as we listen to Him speak in His Word; it happens as we pray. But it also happens as we simply enjoy His presence—meditating on His goodness, delighting in the beauty of His creation, rejoicing in the life of a new baby or the surprise of an unexpected blessing. The Bible says, "Be still, and know that I am God" (Ps. 46:10).

Someday we will be in His presence forever; the Bible says, "God Himself will be with them" (Rev. 21:3). What joy that will be! But in the meantime, delight in His presence right now, for He is with you every hour of the day.

January 17

SERVING ETERNALLY

You have a better and an enduring possession
for yourselves in heaven.
HEBREWS 10:34

Some people think Heaven will be dull and boring, but nothing could be further from the truth. The Father's house will be a happy home because there will be work to do there. John wrote in Revelation 22:3, "His servants shall serve Him." Each one will be given exactly the task that suits his powers, his tastes, and his abilities.

And the Father's house will be a happy home because friends will be there. Have you ever been to a strange place and had the joy of seeing a familiar face? Not one of us who enters the Father's house will feel lonely or strange, for we who have put our trust in Christ are part of His family, sharing Heaven's joys forever with all our brothers and sisters in Christ.

Alexander Maclaren described Heaven this way: "The joys of heaven are not the joys of passive contemplation, of dreamy remembrance, . . . but they are described thus, 'They rest not night or day,' and 'His servants serve Him and see His face.'" In the midst of earth's turmoil, keep your eyes on Heaven!

January 18

GOD'S PRESENCE

*I am with you always,
to the very end of the age.*

MATTHEW 28:20, NIV

These words are Christ's promise to all His disciples, and it is a promise that is marvelously inclusive. No situation is excluded; no challenge is omitted.

Dr. Handley Moule, the noted Greek scholar and Anglican Bishop of Durham (England) in another generation, maintained that the word *always* could be paraphrased to mean, "I am with you all the days, all day long." That means we can count on Christ's presence not only every day, but every moment of every day.

Of the *fact* of His presence there can be no doubt, for His Word cannot fail. What we need is to cultivate the *sense* of His presence, every day, every hour, every moment. This happens as we speak to Him in worship and prayer, and listen to Him speak to us through His Word, the Bible.

January 19

THE TUG OF GOD'S LOVE

The Spirit Himself bears witness with
our spirit that we are children of God.
ROMANS 8:16

Whenever anyone asks me how I can be so certain about who and what God really is, I am reminded of the story of the little boy who was out flying a kite. It was a fine day for kite flying, the wind was brisk and large billowy clouds were blowing across the sky. The kite went up and up until it was entirely hidden by the clouds.

"What are you doing?" a man asked the little boy.

"I'm flying a kite," he replied.

"Flying a kite?" the man said. "How can you be sure? You can't see the kite."

"No," said the boy, "I can't see it, but every little while I feel a tug, so I know for sure that it's there!"

Don't take anyone else's word for God. Find Him for yourself by inviting Jesus Christ to come into your life. Then you, too, will know by the wonderful, warm tug on your heartstrings that He is there *for sure.*

REST FOR THE WEARY

*Come to Me, all you who labor and are
heavy laden, and I will give you rest.*
MATTHEW 11:28

Few people know how to rest these days. Even on vacation, many people rush to cram in as much as they can before returning to their jobs, where they spend twice as much energy catching up on the work and mail that has piled up in their absence. Many of us need vacations just to rest from our vacations! Perhaps we have been looking for rest in the wrong places.

Jesus said "Come to me . . . and I will give you rest." Like peace, rest and contentment can be found only in one place, from one source, and that is the Lord Jesus Christ.

Jesus gives us the ultimate rest, the confidence we need, to escape the frustration and chaos of the world around us. Rest in Him and don't worry about what lies ahead. Jesus Christ has already taken care of tomorrow.

January 21

Keep on Being Filled

Be filled with the Spirit.
Ephesians 5:18, niv

The command to "be filled with the Spirit" actually has the idea of *continuously* being filled in the original Greek language. We are not filled once for all, like a bucket. Instead, we are to be filled constantly. This verse might be translated, "Be filled and keep on being filled."

Dr. Merrill C. Tenney has compared this to the situation of an old-time farmhouse kitchen. In one corner was a sink; above it was a pipe through which came a continuous stream of water from the spring outside. The water, by running constantly, kept the sink brimful of good water.

In the same way, we are not to let ourselves be filled and then emptied of the Spirit—like a leaky bucket—only to be refilled later on, again and again. Rather, the Holy Spirit should flow within us constantly—and He will, as we yield ourselves to Christ's presence and power every day.

January 22

CHILDREN OF LIGHT

You, brethren, are not in darkness. . . .
You are all sons of light.
1 THESSALONIANS 5:4–5

The born-again Christian sees life not as a blurred, confused, meaningless mass, but as something planned and purposeful. His eyes have been opened to spiritual truth.

In Christ's first sermon at Nazareth He said that one of the reasons He had come to earth was to preach "recovery of sight to the blind" (Luke 4:18). By nature we are all spiritually blind because of sin. But the Spirit of God helps us see our sin and our helplessness and shows us God's redeeming grace in Christ. The Spirit reveals the truth of Jesus' declaration: "I am the light of the world. He who follows me shall not walk in darkness, but have the light of life" (John 8:12).

In the Bible we are called "children of light and children of the day" (1 Thess. 5:5, NRSV), because it pleased God to share His mysteries and secrets with us. We are no longer in the dark—we know where we came from, we know why we are here, and we know where we are going. In the midst of a world living in spiritual darkness, walk as a child of the light!

January 23

LIFE AFTER DEATH

For to me, to live is Christ, and to die is gain.
PHILIPPIANS 1:21

I have asked a number of scientists questions concerning life after death, and most of them say, "We just do not know." Science deals in formulas and test tubes. But there is a spiritual world science knows nothing about.

Because many do not believe in life after death, their writings are filled with tragedy and pessimism. The writings of William Faulkner, James Joyce, and many others are filled with pessimism, darkness, and tragedy. Sadly, the same was often true of their lives.

How different from Jesus Christ who said, "I am the resurrection and the life. He who believes in Me, though he may die, he shall live. And whoever lives and believes in Me shall never die" (John 11:25-26). Our hope of immortality is based on Christ alone— not on our desires, longings, arguments, or instincts of immortality. And because we know Christ is alive, we have hope—hope for the present and hope for life beyond the grave.

January 24

BECAUSE OF PRAYER

*The effective, fervent prayer of
a righteous man avails much.*
JAMES 5:16

John Knox prayed, and the results caused Queen Mary to say that she feared the prayers of John Knox more than she feared all the armies of Scotland.

John Wesley prayed, and revival came to England, sparing that nation the horrors of the French Revolution.

Jonathan Edwards prayed, and revival spread throughout the American colonies. History has been changed time after time because of prayer. I tell you, history could be changed again if people went to their knees in believing prayer.

Even when times are bleak and the world scorns God, He still works through the prayers of His people. Pray today for revival in your nation, and around the world.

January 25

SUFFERING AND SUCCESS

Whenever you face trials of any kind,
consider it nothing but joy.
JAMES 1:2, NRSV

Before the power of the atom was discovered, science had to devise a way to smash the atom. The secret of the atom's immeasurable and limitless power was in its being crushed.

Some of the most godly people I've ever known were men and women who were called upon to endure great suffering. They could have grown bitter and resentful... yet, because they knew Christ and walked in the joy of His presence every day, God blessed them and turned them into people who reflected Christ.

Dr. Edward Judson, at the dedication of a church in New York City, said, "Suffering and success go together. If you are succeeding without suffering, it is because others before you have suffered; if you are suffering without succeeding, it is that others after you may succeed."

Admittedly it's hard to "count it all joy" when suffering comes. But when it does, ask God to sanctify it and use it to make you steadfast in your faith.

January 26

WHEN CHRIST COMES

*Abide in Him, that when He appears, we may . . .
not be ashamed before Him at His coming.*
1 JOHN 2:28

Almost 2,000 years ago Jesus Christ won the decisive battle against sin and Satan, through His death and resurrection. Satan did his best to defeat God's plans, but he could not win against God's overwhelming power.

Yet the war continues, for although Satan is a defeated foe, he is still alive and does everything he can to block God's work. But when Christ comes again the war will be over. His victory over evil will be complete, and He will usher in an age in which sin and death will no longer rule, and cruelty and suffering will no longer exist.

For you who believe in Jesus Christ, the future is assured. Tomorrow belongs to you! You await the distant trumpet announcing the coming of Jesus Christ. In the meantime let nothing discourage you. Keep your eyes on Christ and live each day as if He were coming tomorrow. After all, He might!

January 27

ABOVE THE DIN

Let this mind be in you which was also in Christ Jesus.
PHILIPPIANS 2:5

We Christians are not to be conformed to this world in the way we think. The world by its advertisements, its conversation, and its philosophy is engaged in a gigantic brainwashing. Not always consciously but sometimes unconsciously, the Christian is beset by secular and worldly propaganda, calling us to live for ourselves and to put things and selfish pleasures ahead of God. The world's sewage system threatens to contaminate the stream of Christian thought.

However, above the din we can hear the voice of Scripture: "Do not be conformed to this world, but be transformed by the renewing of your mind, that you may prove what is that good and acceptable and perfect will of God" (Rom. 12:2).

Time yourself the next time you read the Bible and pray. Compare it to the amount of time you spend watching television or surfing the Internet. Is God getting His share of your time and attention? Is the world shaping your mind—or is Christ?

January 28

BORROWED TROUBLES

Let your requests be made known to God; and the
peace of God . . . will guard your hearts and minds.
PHILIPPIANS 4:7

No troubles distress the mind and wear
upon the nerves like borrowed troubles. As
someone has written, "Worry is an old man
with a bent head, carrying a load of feathers he thinks
is lead."

Worry about what *might* happen makes even
the smallest trouble seem huge. Nervously
anticipating troubles that may never happen can
crush our spirit.

Instead of "borrowing trouble" by constantly
worrying about the future, listen instead to Jesus'
promise: "Peace I leave with you, My peace I give to
you; not as the world gives do I give to you. Let not
your heart be troubled, neither let it be afraid"
(John 14:27).

Whatever is worrying you right now, give it to
Jesus and trust Him to take care of it. Let His peace
replace your worry.

January 29

GLORIOUS RESPONSIBILITIES

If anyone serves Me,
him My Father will honor.
JOHN 12:26

Young people seek adventure and excitement; but youth wants more—it wants something to believe in; it wants a cause to give itself to and a flag to follow. Without a purpose greater than themselves, young people know they will end up with empty hearts and meaningless lives.

The only cause that is big enough to satisfy the yearning of our hearts is the cause of Jesus Christ; and its flag is the blood-stained body that was lifted on the Cross of Calvary for the redemption of the world.

This invitation to discipleship is the most thrilling cause we could ever imagine. Think of it: The God of the universe invites us to become His partners in reclaiming the world for Him! We can each have a part, using the unique gifts and opportunities God has given us.

Christ's call is for us to be His disciples every day. How are you responding to His call?

January 30

LIVING STONES

You also, as living stones, are
being built up a spiritual house.
1 PETER 2:5

I have a friend who lost his job, a fortune, his wife, and his home. But he tenaciously held to his faith in Christ—the only thing he had left. Like Job in the Old Testament, he would not abandon God, no matter what happened. And yet like Job, he couldn't help but wonder why.

One day he stopped to watch some men doing stonework on a huge church. One of them was chiseling a triangular piece of stone.

"What are you going to do with that?" asked my friend.

The workman said, "See that little opening away up there near the spire? Well, I'm shaping this down here so it will fit in up there."

Tears filled my friend's eyes as he walked away, for it seemed that God had spoken through the workman to explain the ordeal through which he was passing, "I'm shaping you down here so you'll fit in up there."

January 31
GODLY THOUGHTS

Be transformed by the renewing of your mind.
ROMANS 12:2

The Bible teaches that our minds are to be brought under the control of Christ. The reason? How we act will be determined by how we think. If God is to change our lives, He must first change our minds.

The human mind cannot be a vacuum. It will be filled either with good or evil. It will be filled either with Christ or with carnality. What will make the difference? It depends on us, and on what we allow to enter our minds.

Negatively, our minds must be turned away from evil. We must be careful what kind of television programs we see, what kind of books we read, the things that occupy our thoughts.

But it isn't enough to put bad thoughts out of our minds. Positively, they must be replaced with good thoughts—thoughts that are shaped by God and His Word, by prayer and worship, by fellowship with other Christians.

Deliberately turn away from every evil thought today and ask God to fill your mind instead with Himself from this moment on.

February

Pray by name for your friends, family, co-workers, and neighbors who don't know Jesus Christ.

February 1

A GLORIOUS OPPORTUNITY

May the glory of the Lord endure forever;
may the Lord rejoice in His works.
PSALM 104:31

C. T. Studd, the famous Cambridge cricketer and missionary pioneer, wrote the following couplet while still a student at Cambridge:
Only one life, 'twill soon be past;
Only what's done for Christ will last.

Life is a glorious *opportunity* if it is used to condition us for eternity. If we fail in this, though we succeed in everything else, our life will have been a failure. There is no escape for the man who squanders his opportunity to prepare to meet God.

You will never live this day again; once it is gone, it is gone forever. How will you spend it—for yourself, or for Christ? Remember: "Only what's done for Christ will last."

February 2

ALWAYS WITH US

*No good thing will He withhold
from those who walk uprightly.*
PSALM 84:11

Many times we make the mistake of thinking that Christ's help is needed only for sickrooms or in times of overwhelming sorrow and suffering. This is not true. Certainly, God is with us in times of distress, and that is a comforting truth. But listen: Jesus wants to be part of *every* experience and *every* moment of our lives.

He went to the wedding at Cana as well as to the home of Mary and Martha when Lazarus died. He wept with those who wept and rejoiced with those who rejoiced. Someone has said, "There are just as many stars in the sky at noon as at midnight, although we cannot see them in the sun's glare."

I seriously doubt if we will ever understand our trials and adversities until we are safely in heaven. Then when we look back we are going to be absolutely amazed at how God took care of us and blessed us even in the storms of life. But God is with us in the good times also, and we should thank Him for them and commit them to Him just as surely as we do the hard times.

February 3

ABOVE THE CLOUDS

Your faithfulness reaches to the clouds.
PSALM 36:5

My home is on a mountain nearly four thousand feet high. Many times we can see below us the clouds in the valley. Some mornings we wake up to find that we are in lovely sunshine, but the valley below is covered with clouds. At other times thunderstorms come up, and we can see the lightning flash and hear the thunder roar down below, while we are enjoying beautiful sunlight and clear skies above.

Many times I have sat on our rustic front porch and watched the clouds below. I have thought of the clouds of discouragement and suffering that temporarily veil the sunlight of God's love from us. Many people live with a cloud hanging over their lives.

The Bible has a great deal to say about clouds, for they sometimes symbolize the spiritual forces that obscure the face of God. But He has not abandoned us. He is still there, and in faith we know we can trust His promise: "I will never leave you nor forsake you" (Heb. 13:5).

February 4

LOVE DEMONSTRATED

*He loved us and sent His Son
to be the propitiation for our sins.*
1 JOHN 4:10

The word *love* is used to mean many different things. We say that we "love" the house that we have just bought or that we "love" a particular vacation spot or that we "love" a peanut butter and jelly sandwich. We also "love" a certain television program, and we "love" our husband or wife. Hopefully we don't love our spouse the same way we love a peanut butter and jelly sandwich!

The greatest love of all, however, is God's love for us—a love that showed itself in action. A friend once observed, "Love talked about is easily ignored, but love demonstrated is irresistible." The Bible says "God demonstrates His own love toward us, in that while we were still sinners, Christ died for us" (Rom. 5:8). Now that is *real* love! How will you respond to His love today?

February 5

LONGING FOR GOD

My heart and my flesh cry out for the living God.
PSALM 84:2

Have you ever been underwater for a period of time that is longer than you had expected? You know, as the time ticks away, how desperate you become to reach the surface and breathe the air. The greater the time you are underwater, the more you long for a breath of air until that desire overwhelms you, and you rush to get to the surface as rapidly as possible. You have no other thoughts but quenching your need for air.

That is what it means to "long for God," to feel unfulfilled without Him. It means we know we desperately need Him, even more than we need air, and we yearn to be filled with His presence. "My heart and my flesh cry out for the living God."

God wants us to be satisfied with nothing less than Himself. And we are never more fulfilled than when we know Him. Ask God to give you a new hunger for Him, so you may become filled with "the fullness of Christ" (Eph. 4:13).

February 6

TRIUMPH AND GLORY

The day of the Lord so comes as a thief in the night.
1 THESSALONIANS 5:2

Christians have no cause to go around wringing their hands, wondering what they will do in the face of the present world situation. The Scripture says that in the midst of persecution, confusion, wars, and rumors of wars, we are to comfort one another with the knowledge that Jesus Christ is coming back in triumph, glory, and majesty.

Many times when I go to bed at night I think that before I awaken Christ may come. Sometimes when I get up and look at the dawn I think that perhaps this is the day He will return.

But until that day, God is still working—and so should we. In a world filled with turmoil and hopelessness, we are to pray, and we are to do all we can to alleviate suffering and bring Christ's love to others. May Jesus' words become true in your life: "Let your light so shine before men, that they may see your good works and glorify your Father in heaven" (Matt. 5:16).

February 7

THE BREAD OF LIFE

He who wins souls is wise.
PROVERBS 11:30

We have bread to give to a hungry world—the Bread of Life, Jesus Christ. People may be so busy feeding on other things that they ignore Him or refuse Him, but we must keep offering Christ to a spiritually dying world.

We have water to give to a thirsting world—the Living Water, Jesus Christ. People may seek to quench the thirst of their souls in a hundred other ways, but we must keep crying out, "Ho, everyone who thirsts, come to the waters" (Isa. 55:1). Sometimes they can't come, and we have to carry it to them.

We must persevere. We must never give up. Christ never gave up, but "became obedient to the point of death" (Phil. 2:8).

All around you are people who hunger and thirst for God, although they may not even realize it. Will you point them to Christ, who alone can satisfy their deepest longings?

THE STORM IS BEHIND US

You have cast all my sins behind Your back.
ISAIAH 38:17

We shall never understand the extent of God's love in Christ at the Cross until we understand that we shall never have to stand before the judgment of God for our sins. All our sins—without exception—were placed on Christ, and He took the judgment we deserve. He finished the work of redemption.

Once while crossing the North Atlantic in a ship, I looked out my porthole when I got up in the morning and saw one of the blackest clouds I had ever seen. I was certain that we were in for a terrible storm. I ordered my breakfast sent to my room and spoke to the steward about the storm. He said, "Oh, we've already come through that storm. It's behind us."

If we are believers in Jesus Christ, we have already come through the storm of judgment. It happened at the Cross. Don't be bound by your guilt or your fears any longer, but realize that sin's penalty has already been paid by Christ—completely and fully.

February 9

POWER TO CHANGE THE WORLD

You are my hope, O Lord God;
You are my trust from my youth.
PSALM 71:5

We still wrestle with the same problems that preoccupied Plato and Aristotle centuries ago: Where did we come from? Why are we here? Where are we going? We search for answers, but the signs all seem to say "no exit."

But the Cross boldly stands against the confusion of our world, a beacon of hope in the midst of darkness and doubt. In the Cross, Christ not only bridged the gap between God and us, but there we find the answers to life's deepest questions. There we discover our true identity: forgiven sinners who now belong to God. There we discover our true destiny: a glorious eternity with God in Heaven. There we discover our true purpose: to love God and serve Him with all our might.

Never underestimate what Christ did for us through the Cross. By it our salvation was won, and by it our lives—and our world—can be transformed. What difference does the Cross make in your life?

February 10

THE MASTER KEY

The Lord our God we will serve,
and His voice we will obey.
JOSHUA 24:24

I knew a wealthy father who refused to get his son a bicycle because the boy's report card showed disgracefully low marks, the yard was not raked, and other assignments had not been carried out. I'm sure the father would not have been wise to lavish gifts upon such a disobedient and ungrateful son. He wasn't being cruel or stingy; he simply knew his son needed to learn responsibility.

God, too, wants us to learn responsibility. Yes, we are saved by His grace—but we are also called to be responsible disciples, learning to follow Christ by obeying God's will. The Bible warns, "If you do not obey the voice of the LORD, but rebel against the commandment of the LORD, then the hand of the LORD will be against you . . ." (1 Sam. 12:15).

If you want God to hear your prayers, surrender your selfishness and stubbornness to Him, and then humbly seek His will. Obedience is the master key to effective prayer.

February 11

NOT FAITH BUT SIGHT

The Son of man will come in the
glory of His Father with His angels.
MATTHEW 16:27

Today Christ is hidden from our view (although through the Holy Spirit He lives in our hearts). Today is the day of faith; as Paul wrote, "We walk by faith, not by sight" (2 Cor. 5:7). Only in the future will we "see Him as He is" (1 John 3:2).

Christ's first appearing was quiet, almost unnoticed—a humble manger, simple shepherds, an insignificant corner of the Roman Empire. His second appearing will be glorious and universal. He will be accompanied by His angels and will defeat every enemy until He subdues the whole earth.

How easily the events of the moment crowd out the promise of eternity! The present seems so real; the unseen future seems so illusory. But in reality the opposite is true. Don't let the present consume you. Instead, "seek those things which are above, where Christ is" (Col. 3:1).

WE WAIT ON GOD

Those who wait on the Lord shall renew their strength;
they shall mount up with wings like eagles.

ISAIAH 40:31

Nowhere does the Bible teach that Christians are exempt from tribulation and natural disaster. We live in a world infected with the disease of sin, and we share in its misery and pain.

But the Bible does teach that we can face trials with a power others do not have—the power of God. As we trust Him, God helps us endure, and even discern His purposes in the midst of suffering. Christiana Tsai, the Christian daughter of a former governor in China, wrote, "Throughout my many years of illness [53], I have never dared to ask God why He allowed me to suffer so long. I only ask what He wants me to do."

The eagle has the unique ability to lock its joints and soar effortlessly on an updraft, instead of flapping its wings. As we wait on God, He helps us use the winds of adversity to soar above our problems. As the Bible says, "Those who wait on the LORD . . . shall mount up with wings like eagles."

February 13

A Joyful Life

Rejoice in the Lord always.
PHILIPPIANS 4:4

When our hearts are surrendered totally to the will of God, then we delight in seeing Him use us in any way He pleases. Our plans and desires begin to agree with His, and we accept His direction in our lives. Our sense of joy, satisfaction, and fulfillment in life increases, no matter what the circumstances, if we are in the center of God's will.

The Christian life is a joyful life. Christianity was never meant to be something to make people miserable. The ministry of Jesus Christ was one of joy. The Bible teaches that a life of inward peace and outward victory is a Christian's birthright.

"What a witness to the world Christians would be," wrote Amy Carmichael, "if only they were more evidently very happy people." Joy is one of the marks of a true believer. Will others see the joy of Christ in your life today?

CHRISTIAN VIRTUES AT HOME

*I am the vine, you are the branches. He who
abides in Me, and I in him, bears much fruit.*

JOHN 15:5

How we live at home is the acid test for any
Christian man or woman. It is far easier
to live an excellent life among our friends,
when we are putting our best foot forward and are
conscious of public opinion, than it is to live for
Christ in our home.

Our own family circle sees us in our unguarded
moments. They see us when exhaustion and stress fray
our nerves. Our own family circle knows whether
Christ lives in and through us.

If I am a true Christian, I will not give way at home
to bad temper, impatience, faultfinding, sarcasm,
unkindness, suspicion, selfishness, or laziness.
Instead, each day my life will display the fruit of
the Spirit, which is "love, joy, peace, forbearance,
kindness, goodness, faithfulness, gentleness and
self-control" (Gal. 5:22–23, NIV). How different would
your home be if you consistently practiced these
Christ-like virtues?

February 15

Thirsting After Righteousness

They were all filled with the Holy Spirit.
Acts 2:4

The early Christians had no buildings, no airplanes, no automobiles, no printing presses or television or radio. Yet they turned their world "upside down" for Christ. They started a spiritual revolution that shook the very foundations of the Roman Empire.

In the face of opposition and overwhelming odds they stayed courageous, bold, dauntless, and full of faith. They lived their lives daily for Christ, no matter what others thought. They gladly suffered scorn, persecution, and even death for their faith in Christ.

What was their secret? The Bible gives us the key: "They were all filled with the Holy Spirit." The Holy Spirit changed their lives, and those they met couldn't help but be impressed by their love and the quality and purity of their lives. What keeps us from turning our world "upside down" for Christ?

February 16

SERVING GOD FOREVER

Because of His great love ... He ...
made us alive together with Christ.

EPHESIANS 2:4–5

Your life may seem monotonous and filled with drudgery. Yet remember, if you are a Christian, you are not working for an hour or for a day but for eternity. When this body of corruption shall take on immortality, another part of our work will begin, for the Scripture teaches that God's servants shall serve Him forever. The difference is that in Heaven we will never grow bored or weary!

Some time ago a man said to me, "You might be mistaken, for no one has ever come back from the grave to tell us."

I replied, "Sir, that's exactly where you are wrong. Someone has returned—His name is Jesus Christ, our Lord."

That makes all the difference! Because Christ is alive, we have "an inheritance incorruptible and undefiled ... reserved in heaven" (1 Pet. 1:4). And this helps us persevere, even when life seems dull.

February 17

POWER FOR LIFE

The Spirit of truth …
dwells with you and will be in you.
JOHN 14:17

Walter Knight tells the story about a little boy who had recently received Christ. "Daddy, how can I believe in the Holy Spirit when I have never seen Him?" asked Jim.

"I'll show you how," said his father, who was an electrician. The father took Jim to a power plant and showed him the generators. "This is where the power comes from to heat our stove and to give us light. We can't see the power, but it's in that machine and in the power lines," said the father.

"Now, son, let me ask you a question: Do you believe in electricity?" he asked. "Yes, I believe in electricity," said Jim.

"Of course, you do," said his father, "but you don't believe in it because you see it. You believe in it because you see what it can do. Likewise, you can believe in the Holy Spirit not because you see Him, but you see what He does in people's lives when they are surrendered to Christ and possess His power."

February 18

GOD TAKES THE BURDEN

As a father pities his children,
so the Lord pities those who fear Him.

PSALM 103:13

As God's children, we are His dependents. Dependent children spend little time worrying about meals, clothing, and shelter. They assume—and they have a right to—that their parents will provide everything they need.

Jesus said, "Do not worry, saying, 'What shall we eat?' or 'What shall we drink?' or 'What shall we wear?' . . . But seek first the kingdom of God . . . and all these things shall be added to you" (Matt. 6:31, 33).

Unfortunately, worry is an ingrained habit for most of us. But because we are God's children, He is responsible for our welfare. That is why you should be "casting all your care upon Him, for He cares for you" (1 Pet. 5:7). In other words, let God do the worrying! He says, "I'll take the burden—don't give it a thought—leave it to Me."

Never forget: God is bigger than your problems. Whatever worries press upon you today, put them in God's hands—and leave them there.

February 19

A FORMULA FOR PEACE

Great peace have those who love Your law,
and nothing causes them to stumble.
PSALM 119:165

God has a plan for peace, and it is found in His Son, whom the Bible calls the "Prince of Peace" (Isa. 9:6). But we have rejected God's plan. Wars still ravage our world—and our lives.

Why? Jesus said the problem is within us: "Out of the heart . . . proceed evil thoughts, adulteries, fornications, murders, thefts, covetousness, wickedness, deceit, lewdness, an evil eye, blasphemy, pride, foolishness" (Mark 7:21–22). What a list! Our real war is a rebellion against God—and it brings unending misery.

But God longs to see this rebellion cease. That is why Christ came. By His death He provided the way for us to be reconciled to God. And when we have peace with God, we have peace in our hearts—and peace with each other.

This happens as we repent and receive Christ. The war is over, for God extends a peace treaty to all who come to Christ.

A Warning Light

If your heart is wise, My heart will rejoice.
Proverbs 23:15

One of the ways God has revealed Himself to us is in the conscience. Conscience has been described as the light of the soul. Even when it is dulled or darkened by sin, it can still bear witness to the reality of good and evil, and to the holiness of God.

What causes this warning light to go on inside me when I do wrong? It is my conscience, given by God to steer me away from evil and toward good. Conscience can be our gentlest teacher and friend—and sometimes our worst enemy (or so we think) when we sin.

The Scripture says, "Man's conscience is the lamp of the eternal" (Prov. 20:27, MOFFATT). In other words, conscience is God's lamp within the human breast. In his *Critique of Pure Reason,* Immanuel Kant said there were just two things that filled him with awe—the starry heavens above and human conscience within.

Persistent sin can dull or even silence our conscience. On the other hand, persistent attention to God's Word will sharpen our conscience and make us more sensitive to moral and spiritual danger. Is this happening in your life?

February 21

PRAY ANYWHERE, ANY TIME

Rejoice always, pray without ceasing.
1 THESSALONIANS 5:16–17

Prayer is an essential part of a healthy Christian life. Just as omitting an essential vitamin from our diet will make us physically weak, so a lack of prayer will make us spiritually anemic.

The Bible says, "Pray without ceasing." It isn't enough to get out of bed in the morning, quickly bow our head, and repeat a few sentences. Instead, we need to set aside specific times to be alone with God, speaking to Him in prayer and listening to Him speak through His Word. If you set aside special times for prayer, your unconscious mind will be saturated with prayer all day long.

For the overworked mother or other busy person this may seem impossible (although even a few minutes alone with God can reap rich rewards). But even when we are busy, we can "pray without ceasing" in our hearts and minds. We can pray anywhere, any time—and God will hear us. Today let prayer saturate your life "without ceasing."

February 22

TRUST CROWDS OUT WORRY

Commit your way to the Lord . . .
and He shall bring it to pass.
PSALM 37:5

You cannot stop a baby's cry by giving him a rattle when he is hungry. He will keep on crying until his hunger is satisfied by the food his little body demands. Neither can the soul of a mature person be satisfied apart from God. David described the hunger of every human being when he said: "As the deer pants for the water brooks, so pants my soul for You, O God" (Ps. 42:1).

Two conflicting forces cannot exist in one human heart. When doubt reigns, faith cannot abide. Where hatred rules, love is crowded out. Where selfishness rules, there love cannot dwell. When worry is present, trust cannot crowd its way in.

In the same way, God will not share His rightful place in our lives with anything or anyone less than Himself. Is anything crowding God out of your heart today? Don't give first place to anything less than Christ, but "commit your way to the LORD."

February 23

LET IT SHINE!

The light of the righteous rejoices....
PROVERBS 13:9

We are holding a light. We are to let it shine! Though it may seem but a twinkling candle in a world of blackness, it is our business to let it shine. Light dispels darkness, and it attracts people in darkness to it.

We are blowing a trumpet. In the din and noise of battle the sound of our little trumpet may seem to be lost, but we must keep sounding the alarm to those who are in spiritual danger.

We are kindling a fire. In this cold world full of hatred and selfishness our little blaze may seem to be unavailing, but we must keep our fire burning.

A light, a trumpet, a fire ... they seem so little amidst the darkness and violence of the world. But "with God all things are possible" (Matt. 19:26), and He will bless our efforts to bring the good news of Jesus to a weary and strife-torn world.

February 24

No Bargain, No Barter

*Come, buy, . . . without money
and without price.*

ISAIAH 55:1

God does not bargain with us, nor can we barter with Him. He holds our eternal salvation in His omnipotent hand, and He bids us take it as a free gift, "without money and without price."

Yet this is hard for us to accept. Surely something as precious as salvation must cost us greatly! Surely God must demand we work for it!

But that is wrong—and the reason is because the price has already been paid! Salvation is free—but it wasn't cheap. It cost the dear Son of God His very life.

Only cheap, tawdry things have a price tag on them. The best things in life are free—the air we breathe, the stars at night, the wonder of human love. But the greatest gift of all is our salvation, purchased for us by Jesus Christ. "Thanks be to God for His indescribable gift!" (2 Cor. 9:15).

February 25

The Divine Flame

*You shall receive power when the Holy Spirit
has come upon you; and you shall be my witnesses.*
Acts 1:8

Simon Peter was so spiritually weak before
Pentecost that, in spite of his bragging to the
contrary, he swore and denied Christ. He was
cowed by the crowd, shamed by a little maid, and
took his place with the enemies of Christ.

But see him after he has been baptized with fire—
the fire of the Holy Spirit! He stands boldly before
the same rabble that had crucified Jesus, looks into
their faces, and fearlessly proclaims the good news
of salvation (see Acts 2:36). Peter, the weak, was
transformed into Peter, the rock.

So it was with the early disciples. The Holy Spirit
changed them from ordinary individuals into
firebrands for God. Their faith and zeal started
a conflagration that spread throughout the
Roman Empire.

Their secret? Total submission to Jesus Christ and
His will. What keeps you from being used of God to
touch your world for Christ?

February 26

THE HAND OF GOD

*No good thing will He withhold
from those who walk uprightly.*

PSALM 84:11

In the midst of sorrow and trouble, this life has
many blessings and enjoyments that have come
from the hand of God.

Think of the blessings we so easily take for
granted: Life itself; preservation from danger;
every bit of health we enjoy; every hour of liberty;
the ability to see, to hear, to speak, to think, and to
imagine—all this comes from the hand of God. Even
our capacity to love is a gift from God. Most of all,
God has given us the gift of Christ.

What should our response be? We can put it in one
word: *gratitude*. But how do we show our gratitude?
By giving back to Him a part of what He has given us.

What have you done lately to show your gratitude
to God for all that He has done, and is doing, for you?

February 27

A Prepared Place

In my Father's house are many mansions.
JOHN 14:2

As much as our homes mean to us, they are not permanent. Sometimes I look at my own adult children and can hardly believe they are all grown and on their own. The house that once rang with the laughter of children now seems empty.

Those disciples who for Christ's sake gave up houses and lands and loved ones knew little of home life or home joys. It was as if Jesus were saying to them, "We have no lasting home here on earth, but my Father's house is a home where we will be together for all eternity."

The venerable Bishop Ryle is reputed to have said, "Heaven is a prepared place for a prepared people, and those who enter shall find that they are neither unknown or unexpected."

Even life's happiest experiences last but a moment, yet Heaven's joy is eternal. Someday we will go to our eternal Home—and Christ will be there to welcome us!

February 28

A PASSION TO PLEASE GOD

I have learned in whatever state I am, to be content.
PHILIPPIANS 4:11

Popularity and praise can be far more dangerous for the Christian than persecution. They can turn us away from God without our even being aware of it, making us like those in Jesus' day who "loved the praise of men more than the praise of God" (John 12:43).

Unfortunately, it is easy when all goes well to lose our perspective. Instead, we must learn like Paul to be content in whatever state we find ourselves.

The important thing is to have one consuming passion: to please Christ. Then, whatever happens, we know He has permitted it to take place to teach us and to perfect us for His service. He will enrich our circumstances, be they pleasant or disagreeable, by His presence with us.

Ask God to keep you from worrying about what others think, and to be content with whatever He sends your way. All the tomorrows of our lives have to pass Him before they get to us!

March

*Pray for opportunities to deepen
relationships with those you know
who need a relationship
with Jesus Christ.*

March 1

IN THE WORLD, NOT OF THE WORLD

They are of the world. . . . We are of God.
1 JOHN 4:5–6

The Gulf Stream flows in the ocean, and yet it is not absorbed by it. It maintains its warm temperatures even in the icy waters of the North Atlantic.

Believers are in the world, and yet they must not be absorbed by it. If Christians are to fulfill their purposes in the world, they must not be chilled by the indifferent, godless society in which they live. The Bible says, "Do not be conformed to this world" (Rom. 12:2). It is true that Jesus dined with publicans and sinners, but He did not allow the social group to overwhelm Him and conform Him to its ways. Instead, He seized every opportunity to present spiritual truth and to lead a soul from death to life.

Our social contacts should not only be pleasant, they should be opportunities to share our faith with those who do not yet know Christ. As you have contact with others this day, will they sense the warmth of Christ's presence through you?

March 2

PEOPLE OF PRAYER

Lord, teach us to pray.
LUKE 11:1

Thousands pray only in times of great stress, danger, or uncertainty. I have flown through bad storms and found myself surrounded by people praying for the first time in their lives. It is instinctive for us to pray in times of trouble. Only then do we realize our helplessness.

But Christ instructed His followers to pray at *all* times, both by His teaching and His example. So fervent and so direct were His prayers that once, after He finished praying, His followers pleaded, "Lord, teach *us* to pray" (Luke 11:1). They yearned to be in touch with God, as they knew Christ was.

Have you ever said, "Lord, teach *me* to pray?" Prayer shouldn't be casual or sporadic, dictated only by the needs of the moment. Prayer should be as much a part of our lives as breathing. Never has our world stood in greater need of people who will pray. Will you be one of them?

March 3

WE CAN COUNT ON HIM

Blessed is the man whose strength is in You.
PSALM 84:5

Someone has written a little verse that goes:

Said the robin to the sparrow,
I should really like to know,
Why these anxious human beings
Rush about and worry so.
Said the sparrow to the robin,
Friend, I think that it must be,
That they have no heavenly Father
Such as cares for you and me.

Jesus used the carefree attitude of the birds to underscore the fact that worrying is unnatural. "Look at the birds of the air, for they neither sow nor reap; . . . yet your heavenly Father feeds them" (Matt. 6:26). If He cares for tiny birds and frail flowers, why can't we count on Him for every aspect of our lives? After all, He loves us so much that He sent His Son into the world to save us. We are that valuable to Him!

March 4

LIFE PLUS LOVE

All the law is fulfilled in one word;
. . . love your neighbor as yourself.
GALATIANS 5:14

S uppose I gave everything I had to charity. You probably would say I was a very good person—a fine Christian. But Paul said that unless I acted out of love, "I am nothing" (1 Cor. 13:2). George Sweeting has said, "Life minus love equals nothing!"

Do you have this kind of love—a love that puts others ahead of yourself? Without Jesus Christ in your heart, without the Holy Spirit in your life, you can't produce this love. This is the kind of love Jesus had for us, when He willingly left the glory of Heaven and went to the cross for our salvation.

Only God can give us a selfless love for others, as the Holy Spirit changes us from within. This is one reason we must receive Christ, for apart from His Spirit we can never be freed from the chains of selfishness, jealousy, and indifference. Will others see Christ's love in your life today?

March 5

THE SPIRIT OF GOD

I will pray the Father, and He will give you another Helper, that He may abide with you forever.
JOHN 14:16

During His lifetime on earth, Christ's presence could be experienced only by a small group of people at any given time. Now Christ dwells through the Spirit in the hearts of all who have received Him as Savior and Lord. The apostle Paul wrote, "Do you not know . . . that the Spirit of God dwells in you?" (1 Cor. 3:16).

The Holy Spirit is given to every believer—not for a limited time, but forever. If He left us for one moment, we would be in deep trouble. But He doesn't!

He is there to give you both the gifts and the power to work for Christ. He is there to give you strength in the moment of temptation. He is there to produce the fruit of "love, joy, peace, longsuffering, kindness, goodness, faithfulness, gentleness, self-control" (Gal. 5:22–23).

You will never have more of the Holy Spirit than you do right now. But will He have more of you?

March 6

GLORIOUS GIVING

Give, and it will be given to you.
LUKE 6:38

"Give," Christ commanded. Yet it was more than a command. It was an invitation to glorious and abundant living. If a person gets his attitude toward money right, it will help straighten out almost every other area of his life.

Have you ever realized just how cruel and deceptive a master money can be? Some people spend their entire lives slavishly serving it—often without even realizing it. No wonder Jesus warned, "You cannot serve both God and money" (Matt. 6:24, NIV).

The chief motive of the selfish, unregenerate person is "get." The chief motive of the dedicated Christian should be "give." Jesus said, "Give, and it will be given to you." It's a promise, and we know Jesus never breaks His promises.

Getting . . . or giving? Which is true of you?

March 7

LIFE IN CHRIST WORKS

I know whom I have believed.
2 TIMOTHY 1:12

Does Christianity work? Does anything really happen when a person repents of sin and receives Christ by faith?

I can only tell you that it worked in my own life. I was reared during the Depression on a farm in North Carolina. My parents weren't able to give me the advantages most young people enjoy today. I grew up in a Christian home, but by the time I was fifteen, I was in full revolt against all religion—against God, the Bible, the church.

But one night I committed my life to Jesus Christ, and He gave me a whole new direction. My grades picked up. My attitude toward others changed. I began to seek God's will instead of my own way. No, I didn't become perfect, but my life was changed.

I have been all over the world, and I have never met anyone who regretted giving his or her life to Christ. And neither will you.

March 8

THE BRIGHTNESS OF GOD'S LOVE

My flesh and my heart fail;
but God is the strength of my heart.
PSALM 73:26

Trouble will not hurt us unless it does what many of us too often allow it to do—harden us, making us sour, bitter, and skeptical. But it need not be this way. Troubles we bear trustfully can bring us a fresh vision of God and a new outlook on life—an outlook of peace and hope.

If we make our troubles an opportunity to learn more of God's love and His power to aid and bless, then they will teach us to have a firmer confidence in His providence. As a result, the brightness of His love will fill our lives.

Learn to trust God with a child-like dependence on Him as your loving Heavenly Father and no trouble can destroy you. In those darkest hours before the Cross Jesus could still say, "I am not alone, because the Father is with Me" (John 16:32).

The same is true for you. Even in that last dark hour of death, when your flesh and your heart fail, you will be able to depend in peace upon Him who "is the strength of my heart and my portion forever."

March 9

THE MIND OF CHRIST

Let this mind be in you which was also in Christ Jesus.
PHILIPPIANS 2:5

Jesus had the most all-encompassing mind this world has ever seen. His convictions were so strong, so unswerving that He was not afraid to mingle with any group, secure in the knowledge that He would not be contaminated or swayed.

Fear makes us unwilling to give voice to our convictions or to listen to those of others—fear of rejection, fear our beliefs will be attacked, fear our faith might be shaken. But if that is the case, perhaps we need to examine just how deep our convictions really are.

Jesus had no such fear, no need to fence Himself off from others for His own protection. He knew the difference between graciousness and compromise, and we would do well to follow His example.

Jesus alone is "the way, the truth, and the life" (John 14:6). Never lose your confidence in the truth of the Gospel! But—like Jesus—may you always be "speaking the truth in love" (Eph. 4:15).

March 10

A MIGHTY FORTRESS

He is my refuge and my fortress;
my God, in Him I will trust.
PSALM 91:2

A refuge is a place safely out of harm's way. A fortress is a fortified building that is virtually impenetrable by conventional means.

Martin Luther wrote a wonderful hymn that says, "A mighty fortress is our God; a bulwark never failing. Our helper He amidst the flood; of mortal ills prevailing." What a statement about the magnificent power and protection of God!

Does God care for you and me? Can we turn to Him in trust and faith when troubles and temptations threaten to overwhelm us? Yes—a thousand times yes! What greater proof do we need than that He sent His Son, Jesus Christ, to die in our place?

March 11

COME BOLDLY

Ask, and it will be given you; seek, and you will find.
MATTHEW 7:7

Children are not bashful about asking for things. They would not be normal if they did not boldly make their needs known. God has said to His children, "Let us . . . come boldly to the throne of grace, that we may obtain mercy and find grace to help in time of need" (Heb. 4:16). God is keenly aware that we are dependent upon Him for life's necessities. It was for that reason that Jesus said, "Ask, and it will be given to you; seek, and you will find; knock, and it will be opened to you" (Matt. 7:7).

What is troubling you today? Is your heart burdened because of some problem that threatens to overcome you? Are you filled with anxiety and worry, wondering what will happen next? Listen—as a child of God through faith in Christ, you can turn these over to Christ, knowing that He loves you and is able to help you. Don't carry your burden any longer, but bring it "boldly to the throne of grace"—and leave it there.

March 12

GOD'S KINGDOM, GOD'S WAY

Your throne, O God, is forever and ever.
PSALM 45:6

Many intellectuals are asking where history is going. Will society get better and better—or will we end up destroying ourselves?

Christ prayed, "Thy kingdom come. Thy will be done in earth, as it is in heaven" (Matt. 6:10, KJV). Someday that prayer—a prayer that you and I often pray—is going to be answered. The last chapter of history will not be written by any human leader, however good or bad. Only God will write it. And write it He will.

Someday, when the human race stands at the edge of the abyss of self-destruction, God will intervene. It may be tomorrow, it may be a thousand years from now. But the outcome is certain—the future belongs to the Kingdom of God.

Never forget: If you belong to the King, you are on the winning side!

March 13

DYNAMIC AND DEDICATED

Stand fast in the Lord.
PHILIPPIANS 4:1

A bar of raw steel may be purchased for a few dollars. But when that bar of steel has been thrust into the fires and processed, when it has been tempered and forged and made into tiny watch springs for expensive watches, it is worth thousands of dollars. Fire and the skilled hands of master artisans made the difference, enhancing the value.

Just as the sun by its heat and light performs a thousand miracles a day in the plant kingdom, God through the refining fire of His Spirit performs a thousand miracles a day in the spiritual realm. His regenerating power can take the dull and ordinary things of our lives—even the burned-out ashes of our past—and forge them into something useful, even beautiful, for His purposes.

March 14

RESCUING ANGELS

The angel of the Lord encamps all around
those who fear Him, and delivers them.
PSALM 34:7

During World War II, Captain Eddie Rickenbacker and his crew ran out of fuel and ditched their B-17 in the Pacific Ocean. For weeks nothing was heard of him, and across the country thousands of people prayed.

Then he returned, and in an article told what had happened. "And this part I would hesitate to tell," he wrote, "except that there were six witnesses who saw it with me. A gull came out of nowhere, and lighted on my head—I reached up my hand very gently—I killed him and then we divided him equally among us. We ate every bit, even the little bones. Nothing ever tasted so good." This gull saved them from starvation.

Years later I asked him to tell me the story personally, because it was through this experience that he came to know Christ. He said, "I have no explanation except that God sent one of His angels to rescue us." We may never see them, but God still sends His angels to surround and protect His children—including you.

March 15

JOYOUS OPTIMISM

My soul shall be joyful in the Lord.
PSALM 35:9

When Jesus Christ is the source of our joy, no words can describe it. It is a joy "inexpressible and glorious" (1 Pet. 1:8, NIV). Christ is the answer to the sadness and discouragement, the discord and division in our world. He can take discouragement and despondence out of our lives and replace them with optimism and hope.

If our hearts have been attuned to God through an abiding faith in Christ, the result will be joyous optimism and good cheer. The reason? Because we know He loves us, and nothing "shall be able to separate us from the love of God which is in Christ Jesus our Lord" (Rom. 8:39).

When our confidence is in Him, discouragement gets crowded out. May that be true in your life today!

RIGHT ON THE BEAM

*Narrow is the gate and difficult
is the way that leads to life.*
MATTHEW 7:14

Once when we were on a flight from Korea to Japan, we ran through a rough snowstorm. When we arrived over the airport in Tokyo, visibility was almost zero so the pilot had to make an instrument landing. I sat up in the cockpit with him and watched him sweat it out as the watchful men in the airport tower guided him in.

I did not want these men to be broad-minded. I did not want them to say to the pilot, "Oh, well, just land any way you want to. We don't think it'll matter what altitude you keep or how fast you land." I knew that our lives depended on their precise instructions.

Just so, when we come in for the landing in the great airport of Heaven, I don't want any broad-minded advice. I don't want anyone to tell me that it doesn't really matter what I believe, as long as I'm sincere—for Jesus said otherwise. I want to come in on the beam, and even though I may be considered narrow-minded here, I want to be sure of a safe landing there. And I *am* sure, because Christ has gone before me and has provided the way.

March 17

UNLOAD YOUR DISTRESS

Casting all your care upon Him,
for He cares for you.
1 PETER 5:7

I've been told that the French translation of this phrase, "Cast all your care upon Him" is "Unload your distresses upon God." Have you ever seen a dump truck get rid of its load? The driver simply pushes a button or pulls on a lever and the heavy load is discharged at the prescribed spot. The truck would be of no use if it carried its burden forever.

We were never meant to be crushed under the weight of care. We can push the button of faith or pull the lever of trust, and our burden is discharged upon the shoulder of Him who said He would gladly bear it. Unload the anxieties of the present moment upon Him, for He cares for you. If He loved you enough to take away the burden of your sins, can't you trust Him to take away every lesser burden as well?

March 18

MATERIAL GODS

*What will it profit a man if he gains the
whole world, and loses his own soul?*

MARK 8:36

The Bible does not condemn money or material possessions. Money and possessions can do great good, when they are used wisely and kept in proper perspective. Some of the great people of the Bible were very rich. Abraham, Isaac, and Solomon were perhaps the richest men of their day.

God's quarrel is not with material goods but with material gods. Materialism has become the god of too many of us. Our material possessions are elevated to the central place in our lives, and we give them the attention only God deserves.

The Bible teaches that preoccupation with material possessions is a form of idolatry. And God hates idolatry. It poisons every other phase of our lives, including our family life.

The problem, the Bible says, is not with money itself, but with our love of money: "The love of money is a root of all kinds of evil" (1 Tim. 6:10). Don't let money, or anything else, take God's rightful place in your life.

March 19

SOARING IN VICTORY

Unless one is born again,
he cannot see the kingdom of God.
JOHN 3:3

In the third chapter of John, Jesus teaches that the new birth is something God does for us, as we yield ourselves to Him and put our faith and trust in Christ. We do not have within ourselves the seed of the new life; this must come from God.

One day an ugly caterpillar climbs into a tree and spins a silky robe about itself. It goes to sleep, and in a few weeks emerges a beautiful butterfly.

So we—discouraged, unhappy, hounded by guilt, confused, depressed, vainly looking for an escape—can come by faith to Christ and emerge a new person. We can be born again! It sounds incredible, even impossible—and yet it is precisely what happens. We become members of God's family, looking forward to our eternal home in Heaven.

Do you feel you are in a cocoon? Turn to Christ and ask Him to give you your beautiful wings so that you might soar above your problems and be victorious over them.

LIFE WITH A CAPITAL "L"

The Son gives life to whom He will.
JOHN 5:21

The moment you come to Christ, the Spirit of God brings the life of God into you and you begin to live. For the first time you begin to live with a capital "L." There's a spring in your step, a joy in your soul, and a peace in your heart. Life has taken on a new outlook.

There's a whole new direction to your life, because now the Spirit of God has implanted within you the very life of God, Himself, who is eternal. And that means you will live as long as God lives!

Too many Christians let themselves get bogged down by the cares and routines of daily living. Don't let that happen to you. Ask God to help you live each day with eternity in view.

March 21

GOD'S GREAT HEART

*Love the Lord your God with all
your heart . . . and your neighbor as yourself.*
LUKE 10:27

Divine love, like a reflected sunbeam, shines down before it radiates out. Unless our hearts are conditioned by the Holy Spirit to receive and reflect the warmth of God's compassion, we cannot love others as we ought.

Jesus wept tears of compassion at the graveside of a friend. He mourned over Jerusalem because its people had lost their sensitivity to God and His Word. His great heart was always sensitive to the needs of others. When challenged to state the most important commandment, He replied, "You shall love the LORD your God with all your heart . . . [and] your neighbor as yourself" (Matt. 22:37, 39).

Jesus' love was more than human compassion, however; it was in the fullest sense divine love, for He was God in human flesh. This is the kind of love He calls us to have—and the kind He will give us as we seek it from Him.

March 22

EARNEST PRAYER

Continue earnestly in prayer,
being vigilant in it with thanksgiving.
COLOSSIANS 4:2

Today we have learned to harness the power of the atom, but very few of us have learned how to develop fully the power of prayer. We have not yet learned that a man can be more powerful on his knees than behind the most powerful weapons ever developed.

We have not learned that a nation is more powerful when it unites in earnest prayer to God than when its resources are channeled into weapons. We have not discovered that the answer to our problems can be through contact with the living God.

Weapons by themselves will not keep us safe or solve the world's problems. Our basic problems are spiritual in nature, and only spiritual solutions will solve them. That is why prayer is so vital, for only God can change the human heart.

Who knows what might happen if millions of believers around the world availed themselves of the greatest privilege this side of Heaven—the privilege of intercessory prayer? Will you be one of them?

March 23

CLAIM A LARGER BLESSING

Through God we will do valiantly.
PSALM 108:13

There are two ways of getting out of a trial. One is to simply try to get rid of the trial, and be thankful when it is over. The other is to recognize the trial as a challenge from God to claim a larger blessing than we have ever had.

Sometimes God removes our trials, and it isn't necessarily wrong to ask Him to do that. But often the trials remain, and when they do, we should accept them and ask God to teach us from them.

As Peter Marshall once put it, "God will not permit any troubles to come upon us, unless He has a specific plan by which great blessing can come out of the difficulty."

It is through the suffering, the tests and trials of life, that we can draw near to God. A. B. Simpson once heard a man say something he never forgot: "When God tests you, it is a good time for you to test Him by putting His promises to the proof, and claiming from Him just as much as your trials have rendered necessary."

THE VICTORIOUS CHIME

I, even I, am the Lord, and besides Me there is no savior
ISAIAH 43:11

It is said that during Napoleon's Austrian campaign his army advanced to within six miles of the town of Feldkirch. It looked as though his men would take it without resistance. But as Napoleon's army advanced toward their objective in the night, the Christians of Feldkirch gathered in their little church to pray. It was Easter eve.

The next morning at sunrise the bells of the village pealed out across the countryside. Napoleon's army, not realizing it was Easter Sunday, thought that in the night the Austrian army had moved into Feldkirch and the bells were ringing in jubilation. Napoleon ordered a retreat, and the battle at Feldkirch never took place. The Easter bells caused the enemy to flee, and peace reigned in the Austrian countryside.

As Easter is celebrated each year, churches and cathedrals around the world will ring their bells—not to sound Christ's death knell but to declare Christ's victory over death. He is the risen Lord, and because of Him our final enemy—death—has been defeated and peace reigns in our hearts!

March 25

THE ANSWER TO FEAR

Do not be afraid.
MATTHEW 28:10

Months after the September 11, 2001, terrorist attacks on New York and Washington, psychiatrists reported that people who lived thousands of miles away from those tragic events were still coming to them, unable to sleep and paralyzed by fear. We live in a world shaken by fear, apprehension, and anxiety.

What is the answer to this stifling fear? After Jesus had been put to death His disciples huddled in fear behind closed doors, filled with uncertainty and despair. But suddenly they found themselves in the presence of their living Lord, and at His first words their fears disappeared: "Peace to you" (Luke 24:36). The answer to our individual fears is found in a personal faith in the living, glorified Lord.

And the answer to collective fear is a corporate faith in the living, glorified Lord. The answer to national and international tensions and fears is for the world to know Him who is alive forevermore. We do not worship a dead Christ. We worship a risen Christ, who has broken the power of sin and death and hell and is alive forevermore. Why then should we fear?

COWARDLY OR COURAGEOUS?

If God is for us, who can be against us?
ROMANS 8:31

The chairman of the history department of one of our great universities once stated his opinion to me, "We have become a nation of cowards." I challenged his statement, but he argued that many people have become reluctant to follow a course if it isn't popular. I had to admit he was right.

Even if deep inside we know it to be right, we draw back because we are afraid of the consequences. If the odds are in our favor, we will take a stand; but if there is any risk involved in standing up for what we know to be right, we will play it safe.

How different from the early Christians! From one end of the Roman Empire to the other they boldly proclaimed the Gospel in the face of hostility, persecution, scorn, and even death. The apostle Paul knew the key: "For God has not given us the spirit of fear, but of power and of love and of a sound mind" (2 Tim. 1:7).

You may never face the same dangers those early Christians did, but don't take the road of cowardice; don't give in to fear. Remember: "If God is for us, who can be against us?" (Rom. 8:31).

March 27

CHRIST IS RISEN

He is not here, but is risen!
LUKE 24:6

Easter Sunday is the most triumphant and joyous day in the calendar of the Christian Church—and it should be!

For many people the resurrection of Jesus Christ is symbolized by new Easter clothes, or the bright color of daffodils and beautiful, white Easter lilies. But most of all, the wonder of His resurrection is symbolized in the hope that beats in the hearts of believers everywhere as they sing triumphantly: "Christ the Lord is risen today."

It is the message "Jesus is alive!" that lifts Christianity out of the category of dead superstitions and archaic religions and makes it the abiding faith of millions. The angel's message is true: "He is not here, but is risen!" And now God's promise is for you: "If you confess with your mouth the Lord Jesus and believe in your heart that God has raised Him from the dead, you will be saved" (Rom. 10:9).

Peace with God

Let the peace of God rule in your hearts.
Colossians 3:15

Science has confirmed what the Bible taught centuries ago: There is a close relationship between our minds and bodies. Proverbs puts it this way: "A cheerful heart is good medicine, but a crushed spirit dries up the bones" (Prov. 17:22, NIV).

But there is also a close relationship between our mental and physical health and the health of our spiritual lives. Guilt, fear, jealousy, bitterness, futility, escapism—these and a host of other problems are spiritual ills, brought about by the disease of sin. Like poison, they can sicken us in mind and body.

But when Christ comes into our lives, He removes our guilt and takes away our fears. He gives us love for others and a new purpose in life. His joy and peace neutralize sin's poison—and that promotes emotional and physical health.

Does that mean our emotional and physical problems will vanish? Not necessarily. But like a spring of pure water, God's peace in our hearts brings cleansing and refreshment to our minds and bodies.

March 29

A PURPOSE AND A POWER

Go quickly and tell... that He is risen from the dead.
MATTHEW 28:7

When Samuel Morse, inventor of the telegraph, sent his first message, he telegraphed these words: "What hath God wrought!"

The greatest news ever sent tells of a far greater event God has wrought: Christ is risen. On that first resurrection day the angel at the tomb delivered the most important message anyone can ever hear: "He is not here; for He is risen" (Matt. 28:6).

When Adam and Eve first sinned, God's warning became a reality: "You shall surely die" (Gen. 2:17). From that moment on, death reigned over the human race—and with it fear, dread, and superstition.

But Christ's resurrection changed all that, bringing hope and salvation to all who put their trust in Him. Listen: Death is a defeated foe! Christ has won the victory. That is why Paul could say, "Thanks be to God, who gives us the victory through our Lord Jesus Christ" (1 Cor. 15:57). Is your confidence in Jesus Christ, the risen Lord?

He Suffered for You

His visage was marred more than any man.
Isaiah 52:14

When Jesus Christ was on the Cross, His blood draining the life from His body, He knew what it was like to be alone and wracked with pain. But Jesus' pain was far more than just physical pain, for He was suffering God's judgment on all the sins of the ages—the greatest darkness of the soul ever known. As the divine Son of God, He was perfect and without sin. But all our sins were placed on Him, and He took the judgment and hell we alone deserve. He died in our place.

Why did Jesus suffer? For you. For me. That we might have eternal life and have His peace in the midst of life's storms. That we might know that He understands our pain and suffering and stands ready to help.

Why did Jesus suffer? Because God loves us. Because God loves *you*, and Christ willingly went to the Cross for *you*. There was no other way for sin's penalty to be paid, and for us to be redeemed. The Cross is the measure of God's love.

How will *you* respond to His love, poured out on the Cross for *you?*

March 31

IT IS FINISHED

He was wounded for our transgressions.
ISAIAH 53:5

On a hill overlooking the harbor of Macao, Portuguese settlers built a massive cathedral. But over time it fell in ruins, except for one wall. On the top of that high, jutting wall, challenging the elements down through the years, was a huge bronze cross.

It is said that when Sir John Bowring saw it, he was moved to write those words familiar to us all: "In the cross of Christ I glory, / Tow'ring o'er the wrecks of time."

When Jesus lifted up His voice and cried, "It is finished," He did not mean His life was ebbing away or God's plan had been foiled. Though death was near, Jesus realized the last obstacle had been hurdled and the last enemy destroyed. He had successfully and triumphantly completed the task of redemption. With the words, "It is finished," He announced that Heaven's door was open.

Kingdoms and empires come and go, but the Cross and all it stands for will always remain, "Tow'ring o'er the wrecks of time."

April

Pray for pastors in your area who are training their churches to be a part of My Hope with Billy Graham, and make sure your church is involved.

April 1

THE LIVING CHRIST

It is no longer I who live, but Christ lives in me.
GALATIANS 2:20

Jesus Christ was crucified between two thieves on a rugged cross on Calvary, just outside Jerusalem. Think of it: The very Son of God came down from Heaven and "humbled Himself and became obedient to the point of death, even the death of the cross" (Phil. 2:8).

Jesus gave His head to the crown of thorns for us. He gave His face to the human spittle for us. He gave His cheeks and His beard to be plucked out for us. He gave His back to the lash for us. He gave His side to the spear for us. He gave His hands and feet to the spikes for us. He gave His blood for us. Jesus Christ, dying in our place, taking our sins on that cross, is God's love in action.

But that's not the end of the story. He rose again, and He is the living Christ. If Christ is not alive, there is no hope for any of us. But He is alive! And because He is, "he is able to save completely those who come to God through him, because he always lives to intercede for them" (Heb. 7:25, NIV). Hallelujah!

April 2

A LIVING SACRIFICE

Present yourselves to God as being alive ..., and your
members as instruments of righteousness to God.
ROMANS 6:13

The apostle Paul, who was a splendid example of a disciplined Christian, said, "I beseech you therefore, brethren, by the mercies of God, that you present your bodies a living sacrifice, holy, acceptable unto God, which is your reasonable service" (Rom. 12:1, KJV).

If we have given ourselves to Christ, then He has come to live within us, and our bodies are now the temples—the dwelling places—of the Holy Spirit. Now we must act worthy of Him who lives within us, disciplining both our bodies and minds so we do not bring dishonor to Him. We must pray as Jeremy Taylor once prayed, "Let my body be a servant of my spirit, and both body and spirit servants of Jesus."

Paul knew Christ had sacrificed His body for his salvation, and the only reasonable thing to do in response was to give his body as a living sacrifice to Christ.

Let me challenge you to commit your body and your mind to Christ, "which is your reasonable service."

April 3

THE RESURRECTION AND LIFE

The one who believes in me will live, ...
and ... will never die.
JOHN 11:25–26, NIV

We have three great enemies: sin, Satan, and death. Because Christ rose from the dead, we know that sin and death and Satan have been decisively defeated. And because Christ rose from the dead, we know there is life after death, and that if we belong to Him we need not fear death or hell.

Jesus said, "I am the resurrection and the life. The one who believes in me will live, even though they die; and whoever lives by believing in me will never die" (John 11:25–26, NIV). He also promised, "If I go and prepare a place for you, I will come back and take you to be with me that you also may be where I am" (John 14:3, NIV).

How hopeless our lives would be if these words were not true. Every cemetery and every grave site would be a mute witness to the futility and despair of human life. But His words are true! By God's power Jesus rose from the dead and hundreds became witnesses to His resurrection (see 1 Cor. 15:1–8).

What a glorious hope we have because Jesus is alive!

REFINED AND PURIFIED

When He has tested me, I shall come forth as gold.
JOB 23:10

Affliction can be a means of refining and of purification. Just as ore must pass through the refiner's furnace before it can yield up its gold, so our lives must sometimes pass through God's furnace of affliction before they can bring forth something beautiful and useful to Him.

We might never have had the songs of Fanny Crosby had she not been afflicted with blindness. George Matheson would never have given the world his immortal song, "O Love That Will Not Let Me Go," had it not been for the pain of personal tragedy and heartache. The "Hallelujah Chorus" was written by Handel when he was poverty-stricken and suffering from a paralyzed right side and right arm.

Affliction can also make us stronger in our faith and develop our confidence in God's watch care over us. It may also drive us back to the right path when we have wandered. David said, "Before I was afflicted I went astray, but now I keep your word" (Ps. 119:67).

Whatever the reason, if God sends affliction your way, take it in faith as a blessing not a curse.

April 5

THE LIGHT OF GOD'S LOVE

O Lord my God, You are very great;...
You who laid the foundations of the earth.
PSALM 104:1, 5

God's love did not begin at Calvary. Before the morning stars sang together, before the world was baptized with the first light, before the first blades of tender grass peeped out, God was love.

Turn back to the unwritten pages of countless eons before God spoke this present earth into existence, when the earth was "without form and void" and the deep, silent darkness of space stood in stark contrast to the brilliance of God's glory and His cherubim and seraphim.

Even then, God was love. Before the worlds were created, He knew all about us and the need we would have someday for Christ to die for us. So in His love "he chose us in him before the creation of the world" (Eph. 1:4, NIV).

God does not change—and neither does His love. He loved you before you were born . . . He loves you now . . . and He will love you forever. Will you love Him in return?

April 6

THE FUTURE LIFE

As for man, his days are like grass;
as a flower of the field, so he flourishes.
PSALM 103:15

The Bible reminds us that our days are as grass. For a brief time we flourish, but soon we wither and die. Yet the minutes of our lives can be flecked with the gold of eternity. Instead of wasting them—as we so easily do—God exhorts us to redeem the time.

But our lives are also immortal. God made us different from the other creatures. He made us in His own image, a living soul. Don't let anyone tell you that we are simply a higher species of animal. If you believe that, you will begin to act like one. No! You are far greater.

One thousand years from this day you will be more alive than you are at this moment. The Bible teaches that life does not end at the cemetery. There is a future life with God for those who put their trust in His Son, Jesus Christ. There is also a future hell of separation from God where all are going who have refused, rejected, or neglected to receive His Son, Jesus Christ.

Make sure of your relationship to Christ, and then ask God to help you live each day for His glory.

April 7

WE CAN'T OUT-GIVE GOD

The generous soul will be made rich.
PROVERBS 11:25

The Bible teaches that blessings follow those who give liberally. Proverbs 11:25 says, "The generous soul will be made rich, and he who waters will also be watered himself."

I've heard countless testimonies from men and women who were afraid to put to the test God's promise to bless those who are generous. They feared they would not have enough. Then, when at last they decided to tithe (to give a tenth of their income) in accordance with the Bible's standard, they began to prosper. They discovered what countless others have known across the ages: You can't out-give God.

What keeps you from being more generous in supporting God's work? Selfishness? Fear? Insecurity? Even a sinful habit you would rather support? Whatever the reason, repent of it and discover the blessedness of generosity. Remember: "God loves a cheerful giver" (2 Cor. 9:7).

April 8

GOD CARES FOR YOU

God is not the author of confusion but of peace.
1 CORINTHIANS 14:33

Who of us has not asked in times of affliction and difficulty—does God care for me? The Psalmist said, "Refuge failed me; no man cared for my soul" (Ps. 142:4, KJV). Martha, over-concerned with her workaday duties, said to Jesus, "Lord, do You not care?" How many faithful, loving mothers, overwhelmed by the burdens of motherhood, have cried anxiously, "Lord, do You not care?"

That question is forever answered in those reassuring words of Peter: "He cares for you" (1 Pet. 5:7). This is the Word of God. Even if the world passes away it will not change.

You can be confident God cares for you. If He didn't, would He have sent Christ into the world to die for you? Of course not! That is why you can always turn to Him for the strength and encouragement you need.

Yes, life can be overwhelming at times. But when it is, remember this: God knows what you are facing, and "He cares for you."

April 9

THE GOOD SHEPHERD

The good shepherd lays down his life for the sheep.
JOHN 10:11, NIV

One of the figures of speech Jesus applied to Himself was that of a shepherd. He said, "I am the good shepherd. The good shepherd lays down his life for the sheep. The hired hand is not the shepherd who owns the sheep.... I know my sheep and my sheep know me" (John 10:11–14, NIV).

Note four things about Jesus, the Good Shepherd. He *owns* the sheep; they belong to Him. Next, He *guards* the sheep; He never abandons them when danger approaches. Also, He *knows* the sheep; He calls them by name and they follow Him. Finally, He *lays down His life* for the sheep; their salvation is His primary concern.

The Bible says, "We are His people and the sheep of His pasture" (Ps. 100:3). Because we belong to Christ, we can be secure and at rest.

April 10

THE MESSAGE OF EASTER

He has risen! He is not here.
MARK 16:6, NIV

The message of Easter is the central focus of Christianity.

The apostle Paul said, "If Christ has not been raised, your faith is futile; you are still in your sins" (1 Cor. 15:17, NIV). It is as simple as that. If Christ is still dead, then He cannot be our Savior, for He was not the Son of God, and He died like all men. More than that, Heaven's doors are still locked.

But if Christ is risen, as the Scriptures teach and as hundreds of witnesses testified (none of whom ever recanted that testimony despite threats and death for many of them), then we have the ultimate hope of humanity—eternal life with the God who made us and the certainty of life beyond the grave.

What does Easter mean to you? It should mean everything, because Christ has conquered death! And that makes all the difference—now and forever!

April 11

RISEN AND RETURNING

This same Jesus . . . will so come in
like manner as you saw Him go.
ACTS 1:11

The resurrection of Jesus Christ is the key to God's plan for the future. Unless Christ was raised from the dead, there can be no future kingdom and no returning King. Unless Christ was raised from the dead, sin and death still reign, and God's plan of redemption remains unfulfilled. But Christ *has* been raised!

As the disciples stood watching after Jesus ascended into the heavens, the angels assured them that the risen Christ would someday be the returning Christ. "Men of Galilee, why do you stand gazing up into heaven? This same Jesus, who was taken up from you into heaven, will so come in like manner as you saw Him go into heaven" (Acts 1:11).

Just as surely as Christ rose from the dead, so He will return and take us to Himself. Every promise—without exception—will be fulfilled.

April 12

A Certain Hope

Blessed is the man who trusts in the Lord,
and whose hope is the Lord.

JEREMIAH 17:7

One of the great hymns of the church, "The Solid Rock," by Edward Mote and William Bradbury, begins, "My hope is built on nothing less, than Jesus' blood and righteousness; I dare not trust the sweetest frame, but wholly lean on Jesus' name. On Christ, the solid Rock, I stand; all other ground is sinking sand."

On what is your hope built? You may hope for a raise in pay at work. You may hope that you pass an exam at school. You may even hope that you win a contest you have entered. Such hopes are based on externals over which we have little control: a favorable view of our work by the boss, the "right" questions being asked by the professor, our name being drawn among thousands of entries.

But all these "hopes" fade into insignificance when compared with the greatest hope of all—our hope of salvation in Christ. And that hope is an absolute certainty, because it is based not on ourselves or our good works, but squarely on "Jesus' blood and righteousness."

April 13

WHY DID HE DIE?

The message of the cross . . . is the power of God.
1 CORINTHIANS 1:18

We can never grasp the horror of human sin until we realize it caused the Son of God to be crucified. Not Pilate, not Judas, not the mob—but sin.

The ravages of war and poverty, the wrenching pain of loneliness and rejection. The haunting cry of the orphan and widow, the dying gasps of the world's starving—these and a thousand other tragedies all bear witness to the fact that we live in a world poisoned by sin.

And that is why Jesus died. The terrible, bitter cup of humanity's sin sent Him to the Cross. Jesus prayed in those last hours, "O, My Father, if it is possible, let this cup pass from Me; nevertheless, not as I will, but as You will" (Matt. 26:39). There was no other way. Why did He drink that awful cup? So you and I would not have to.

Sin is the second most powerful force in the universe, for it sent Jesus to the Cross. Only one force is greater—the love of God.

April 14

Forgiveness and Fellowship

I will forgive their iniquity,
and their sin I will remember no more.

Jeremiah 31:34

There is no possibility of true happiness until we have established friendship and fellowship with God. And there is no possibility of establishing this fellowship apart from the Cross of His Son, Jesus Christ.

God says, "I will forgive you, but I will forgive only at the foot of the Cross." He says, "I will fellowship with you, but I will fellowship with you only at the Cross."

Why is this? Because only through Christ's death on the Cross can we be forgiven and reconciled to God.

This is why we must come to the Cross, repenting of our sins and trusting Christ alone to save us. Human pride gets in the way; we don't want to admit we are sinners, or that we are too weak to save ourselves. Only when we leave our pride at the Cross can our hearts be open to God's redeeming grace.

When we come to Christ, God imparts His righteousness to us. It is as if an accounting entry had been made in the books of Heaven, declaring us righteous for Christ's sake. The Divine Bookkeeper cancels our debt!

April 15

HEAVENLY NEWS

God both raised up the Lord
and will also raise us up by His power.
1 CORINTHIANS 6:14

The angel who came to the garden where Jesus' body lay, rolled away the stone and permitted fresh air and morning light to fill His tomb. The sepulcher was no longer an empty vault or dreary mausoleum; rather it was a life-affirming place that radiated the glory and power of the living God. No longer was the tomb a dark, fearsome prison but a transformed reminder of the celestial light that sweeps aside the shadows of death. Jesus' resurrection changed all that—forever!

An unknown poet has said of the tomb, "'Tis now a cell where angels used to come and go with heavenly news." No words of men or angels can adequately describe the height and depth, the length and breadth of the glory to which the world awakened when Jesus came forth to life from the pall of death.

Jesus' promise has been fulfilled: "Because I live, you will live also" (John 14:19).

April 16

THE GREATEST MESSAGE

I know that you seek Jesus who was crucified.
MATTHEW 28:5

On the third day after Christ's death the Bible says, "And behold there was a great earthquake; for an angel of the Lord descended from heaven, and came and rolled back the stone from the door, and sat on it. His countenance was like lightning, and his clothing as white as snow. And the guards shook for fear of him, and became like dead men" (Matt. 28:2–4).

As Mary looked into the tomb she saw "two angels in white sitting, one at the head and the other at the feet, where the body of Jesus had lain" (John 20:12). Then one of the angels who was sitting outside the tomb proclaimed the greatest message the world has ever heard: "He is not here; for He is risen" (Matt. 28:6). Those few words changed the history of the universe. Darkness and despair died; hope and anticipation were born in the hearts of men.

With those few words joy and new life now dawn in the hearts of all who believe. Don't leave Jesus in the manger . . . or on the Cross . . . or in the tomb. He is alive, and even now He wants to walk beside you every day.

April 17

PATIENCE AND PRAYER

We . . . do not cease to pray for you.
COLOSSIANS 1:9

Some years ago, a woman wrote me that she had pleaded for ten years for the conversion of her husband, but that he was more hardened than ever. I advised her to continue to plead. Sometime later I heard from her again. She said her husband was gloriously and miraculously converted in the eleventh year of her prayer vigil. How thankful she was that she had kept on praying!

The Scripture says, "Pray without ceasing" (1 Thess. 5:17). This should be the motto of every true follower of Jesus Christ. Never stop praying, no matter how dark and hopeless your case may seem. Your responsibility isn't to tell God *when* He must act or even *how* He must act. Your responsibility is simply to "pray without ceasing," trusting Him to act according to His perfect will.

April 18

A Sure Supply

My God shall supply all your need.
PHILIPPIANS 4:19

One lesson that Jesus would teach us is to have confidence that God answers every true petition. Skeptics may question it, humanists may deny it, and intellectuals may ridicule it. Yet here is Christ's own promise: "If you abide in Me, and My words abide in you, you will ask what you desire, and it shall be done for you" (John 15:7).

Does this verse mean God gives us a blank check (so to speak) when we pray? Does He promise to give us anything we want, if we just keep asking? No. God loves us too much to answer prayers that are foolish or might harm us. But the closer we get to Him—the more we abide in Him and His Word abides in us—the more we will desire what He desires, and the more our prayers will reflect His will.

The Bible promises, "No good thing does he withhold from those whose walk is blameless" (Ps. 84:11, NIV). Trust that promise with all your soul.

April 19

SHINING LIGHTS

*Let your light so shine before men,
that they may ... glorify your Father in heaven.*
MATTHEW 5:16

Our Lord regarded His followers as a select company who belonged to a different world from the rest of humanity. Many of the religious people of His day were worldly and unspiritual, publicly parading their religion to impress others while privately dominated by pride, ambition, greed, and falsehood.

Jesus told His disciples they could not make their light shine by sinking to the world's low level. It was only by abiding in Christ and living under the ruling power of His Holy Spirit that they could rise above the world. Only in that way could they be salt and light to a decaying and darkened world.

Our influence on society depends on our likeness to Jesus Christ. We cannot elevate others higher than we ourselves have gone. The first century Christians out-thought, out-lived, and out-loved their neighbors, and by their example of purity and compassion attracted countless thousands to the Christian faith.

What do others see in your life that would attract them to Christ?

April 20

THE CALL TO DISCIPLESHIP

Take my yoke upon you and learn from Me.
MATTHEW 11:29

A generation ago, Jim Elliot went from Wheaton College to become a missionary to the Aucas in Ecuador. Before he was killed, he wrote, "He is no fool who gives what he cannot keep to gain what he cannot lose."

The Christian faith brings its own "blood, sweat, and tears" to those who would follow Jesus Christ. Christ calls us to discipleship. When we come to Him, He takes away one set of burdens—the burden of sin, the burden of guilt, the burden of separation from God, the burden of hopelessness.

But He also calls us to follow Him, to renounce our selfish desires, and seek His will above all else. He calls to us: "Take My yoke upon you and learn from Me."

So are we simply exchanging one burden for another—the burden of sin for the burden of obedience? No! It is no burden to follow Christ. Instead, we become the bearers of joy—because now we are yoked to the very Son of God. Nor is it too heavy to bear, for Christ bears it with us: "My yoke is easy and My burden is light" (Matt. 11:30).

With whom are you yoked—the world or Christ?

April 21

GOD NEVER CHANGES

*God is Spirit, and those who worship Him
must worship in spirit and truth.*
JOHN 4:24

I was reared in a small Presbyterian church in
Charlotte, North Carolina. Before I was ten
years of age my mother made me memorize the
"Shorter Catechism," a summary of basic Christian
beliefs in the form of questions and answers. In the
catechism we were asked to define God. The answer
we learned was, "God is a Spirit—infinite, eternal, and
unchangeable."

Those three words beautifully describe God. He
is infinite—not body-bound. Eternal—He has no
beginning and no ending. He is unchangeable—never
changing, never capricious, never unreliable. As the
Bible says, with God "there is no variation or shadow of
turning" (James 1:17). He is forever self-existent.

People change, fashions change, conditions and
circumstances change, but God never changes. His
love never changes. His holiness never changes. His
purpose never changes. His glory never changes. He is
the same yesterday, today, and forever.

Can you think of any reason *not* to trust Him?
Neither can I!

April 22

THE HOPE OF THE CENTURIES

*It is good that one should hope and
wait quietly for the salvation of the Lord.*

LAMENTATIONS 3:26

The promised coming of Christ has been the great hope of believers down through the centuries. The ancient Nicene Creed affirms, "He shall come again with glory."

Charles Wesley wrote 7,000 hymns; 5,000 mention the coming of Christ. As the Archbishop of Canterbury crowned Queen Elizabeth II, he stated, "I give thee, O Sovereign Lady, this crown to wear until He who reserves the right to wear it shall return."

But until that time, our world remains in the grip of violence and despair. One noted columnist summed it up this way: "For us all, the world is disorderly and dangerous; ungoverned, and apparently ungovernable." Someday, however, the King will return. Someday the heavens will shout, "The kingdoms of this world have become the kingdoms of our Lord and of His Christ, and He shall reign forever and ever!" (Rev. 11:15).

Christ alone is the answer to the burdens of our hearts and the hopelessness of our world.

April 23

COMFORTING OTHERS

Comfort each other and edify one another.
1 THESSALONIANS 5:11

It is an undeniable fact that usually those who have suffered most are best able to comfort others who are passing through suffering. They know what it is to suffer, and they understand more than others what a suffering person is experiencing—physically, emotionally, and spiritually. They are able to empathize as well as sympathize with the afflictions of others because of what they have experienced in their own lives.

Our sufferings may be rough and hard to bear, but they teach us lessons that in turn equip and enable us to help others. Our attitude toward suffering should not be, "Grit your teeth and bear it," hoping it will pass as quickly as possible. Rather, our goal should be to learn all we can from what we are called upon to endure, so that we in turn can "comfort each other and edify one another."

WALK WITH GOD

My eyes shall be on the faithful of the land,
that they may dwell with me.

PSALM 101:6

Walk with God as Noah did; when the flood came, Noah was saved amidst the scorn and rejection of his neighbors. Walk with God as Moses did in the solitude of the desert; when the hour of judgment fell upon Egypt, Moses was prepared to lead his people to victory.

Walk with God as David did as a shepherd boy; when he was called to rule his people he was prepared for the task of kingship.

Walk with God as Daniel and his three young friends did in the palace of Babylon's king; when the fiery furnace and the lion's den came, God was beside them and delivered them.

No, God didn't always deliver His saints from adversity or even death, nor does He today. But because they had learned to trust Him in the light, they were prepared to follow Him in the darkness.

God has not promised to deliver us *from* trouble, but He has promised to go with us *through* the trouble. "Yea, though I walk through the valley of the shadow of death, I will fear no evil; for You are with me" (Ps. 23:4).

April 25

CORONATION DAY

Blessed is the man who endures trial
for ... he will receive the crown of life.
JAMES 1:12, RSV

To the Christian, death is said in the Bible to be a coronation. The picture here is that of a regal prince who, after his struggles and conquests in an alien land, returns to his native country and court to be crowned and honored for his deeds.

The Bible says we are pilgrims and strangers in a foreign land. This world is not our home; our citizenship is in Heaven. And someday all our battles on this earth will be over, and we will enter that Heavenly Home.

To the one who has been faithful Christ will give a crown of life. Paul said, "There is laid up for me the crown of righteousness, which the Lord, the righteous Judge, will give to me on that day, and not to me only but also to all who have loved His appearing" (2 Tim. 4:8).

When D. L. Moody was dying, he looked up to Heaven and said, "Earth is receding, Heaven is opening, this is my coronation day." Never forget: If you are a Christian, you are a child of the King!

April 26

Now Is the Time

You do not know
what will happen tomorrow.
JAMES 4:14

Billy Bray, a godly clergyman of another generation, sat by the bedside of a dying Christian who had been very shy about his testimony for Christ during his life. The dying man said, "If I had the power I'd shout glory to God." Billy Bray answered, "It's a pity you didn't shout glory when you had the power."

I wonder how many of us will look back over a lifetime of wasted opportunities and ineffective witness, and weep because we did not allow God to use us as He wanted. "Night is coming, when no man can work" (John 9:4, NASB).

If ever we are to study the Scriptures, if ever we are to spend time in prayer, if ever we are to win souls for Christ, if ever we are to invest our finances for His kingdom—it must be now.

April 27

CHRIST IS KING

Your kingdom is an everlasting kingdom.
PSALM 145:13

The government in God's kingdom is unique. It is not a democracy where the people govern, but a "Christocracy" where Christ is the supreme authority. In a society of unredeemed people, democracy is the only fair and equitable system. But no democracy can ever be better than the people who make it up. When citizens are selfishly motivated, the government will be inequitable. When people are dishonest, the government will be the same. When everyone wants his own way, someone is going to get hurt.

But in God's kingdom, Christ is King. He is compassionate, fair, merciful, and just. When He is sovereign in men's hearts, anguish turns to peace, hatred is transformed into love, and misunderstanding into harmony.

Is Christ the King of your motives and your attitudes?

A Sealed Bargain

He ... put his Spirit in our hearts as a deposit,
guaranteeing what is to come.
2 Corinthians 1:21–22, niv

As we trust in Christ, God gives us the Spirit as a pledge, or, as some translations read, *earnest* or *guarantee.* "He ... put his Spirit in our hearts as a deposit, guaranteeing what is to come."

In the apostle Paul's day, a deposit or pledge did three things: It was a down payment that sealed a bargain, it represented an obligation to buy, and it was a sample of what was to come.

As an illustration, suppose you decided to make a down payment on a new car. What does your deposit represent? First, it seals the transaction; from now on, both you and the seller are committed. Also, it shows that you have committed yourself to pay the rest of the purchase price. Finally, it enables you to take possession of the car right now (even though it still belongs to the bank!).

In the same way, the Holy Spirit in our hearts is God's pledge or deposit to us—sealing His commitment to save us, guaranteeing that someday our salvation will be complete, and enabling us to experience its joys right now.

April 29

LIVE FOR THE LORD

My days are swifter than a weaver's shuttle.
JOB 7:6

In North Carolina I have visited the textile mills and have watched the giant looms that turn out cloth for the nation. The shuttles move with the speed of lightning, scarcely visible to the naked eye.

Job says that his days are "swifter than a weaver's shuttle." Life passes so quickly it is almost over before we realize it. The Bible says this is the chronology of eternity. Though you live to be seventy, eighty, or ninety years old, that is but a snap of the finger compared to eternity.

Put your hand on your heart and feel it beat. It is saying, "Quick! Quick! Quick!" We have only a few brief years at the most. Let's live them for the Lord.

April 30

THE SECRET OF PURITY

Who shall ascend the hill of the Lord?...
He who has clean hands and a pure heart.
PSALM 24:3–4, RSV

We live in the most permissive society since pagan times. Movie marquees, the covers of magazines, the Internet, billboards, television—all scream sensual messages at us. "If it feels good, do it" has become a national motto.

Yet, if you talk with people who have come to Christ out of deep sin, they will tell you they wish they had never fallen into such sin and that they had come to Christ sooner.

Many Christian books tell of men and women who committed terrible crimes or were entangled in immorality or sensuality. We rejoice with them that Christ has redeemed and forgiven them. But how much better to have avoided such sin in the first place! God's standard has not changed: "You shall be holy, for I the LORD your God am holy" (Lev. 19:2).

The secret of purity is God. When we are committed to Christ, we will shrink back from all that is impure. Instead, we will seek a pure heart—a heart cleansed by the Holy Spirit and the Word of God.

May

*Pray for other Christians to catch
the vision for* My Hope with
Billy Graham *and get involved now.*

May 1

GOD'S KIND OF STRENGTH

They shall walk and not faint.
ISAIAH 40:31

Never in history have the nations of the world possessed so many lethal armaments, so many ways to bring death and destruction to the human race. Some of our most brilliant minds spend their entire lives developing new and more sophisticated ways to destroy life.

But have all our weapons brought us lasting security? On the contrary; if anything, they have made the world less secure. At any one time at least thirty wars rage in various parts of the world, in addition to countless instances of civil unrest. I am reminded of the false prophets of Jeremiah's day: " 'Peace, peace,' they say, when there is no peace" (Jer. 8:11, NIV).

In the midst of an uncertain and threatening world, however, we can have peace. It comes from putting our trust in the living God. Isaiah's words—written in a time of great upheaval—still speak to us today: "Those who wait on the LORD shall renew their strength; . . . they shall walk and not faint" (Isa. 40:31).

May 2

OUR INFINITE GOD

Great is the Lord, and greatly to be praised.
PSALM 48:1

As a boy I grew up in the rural American South. My idea of the ocean was so small that the first time I saw the Atlantic I couldn't comprehend how any lake could be so big! The vastness of the ocean cannot be understood until it is seen.

This is the same with God's love. It passes knowledge. Until you actually experience it, no one can describe its wonders to you. The opening lines of one of our great old hymns declare, "O the deep, deep love of Jesus / Vast, unmeasured, boundless, free! / Rolling as a mighty ocean / In its fullness over me."

Behind the love of God lies His omniscience—His ability to "know and understand all." Omniscience is a quality of God that is His alone. God possesses infinite knowledge and an awareness that is uniquely His. At all times, even in the midst of any type of suffering, I can realize that He knows, loves, watches, understands, and, more than that, has a purpose.

No matter what comes your way . . . no matter how tempted you are to give in to despair . . . never forget: God's love for you can never be exhausted, for His love is beyond measure.

May 3

WALK IN THE SPIRIT

Walk in the Spirit, and you
shall not fulfill the lust of the flesh.
GALATIANS 5:16

To walk means to place one foot in front of the other and to go forward one step at a time. If you stop doing this, you are no longer walking. You are standing still—or worse, going backwards. Walking always implies movement, progress, and direction.

This is what it means to walk with God. It means moving forward in step with Him, confident that the way He is leading is best.

The problem is that we are weak. We stumble or get diverted, or get weary and stop moving forward. But that is one reason why the Holy Spirit has been given to us. Galatians 5:16 could be paraphrased this way: "Walk by means of the Spirit."

One of the highest commendations in the Bible is found in these words about Noah: "Noah was a just man, perfect in his generations. Noah walked with God" (Gen. 6:9). Could this be said of us?

May 4

GOD'S PERFECT PLAN

Be transformed ... that you may prove
what is that ... perfect will of God.
ROMANS 12:2

The Bible reveals that God has a plan for every life, and that if we live in constant fellowship with Him, He will direct and lead us in the fulfillment of this plan.

God does not reveal His plan through fortune-tellers, astrologers, soothsayers, and workers of hocus-pocus. His perfect will is reserved for those who have trusted Christ for salvation. He shares His secrets only with those who are redeemed and transformed, and who humbly seek His will for their lives.

You cannot know the will of God for your life unless you first come to the cross and confess that you are a sinner and receive Christ as Lord and Savior. Once you do come to Him, you begin a whole new life—life not lived for yourself but for Christ. From that moment on God wants to show you His will. Whatever decisions you face today, commit them to God and ask Him to guide you—and He will.

May 5

CONFESSION AND CLEANSING

*If we confess our sins, He is faithful
and just to forgive us our sins.*
1 JOHN 1:9

Corrie ten Boom tells a story of a little girl who broke one of her mother's demitasse cups. The little girl came to her mother sobbing, "Oh, Mama, I'm so sorry I broke your beautiful cup."

The mother replied, "I know you're sorry and I forgive you. Now don't cry any more." The mother then swept up the pieces of the broken cup and placed them in the trash can. But the little girl enjoyed the guilty feeling. She went to the trash can, picked out pieces of the cup, brought them to her mother and sobbed, "Mother, I'm so sorry that I broke your pretty cup."

This time her mother spoke firmly to her, "Take those pieces and put them back in the trash can. Don't be silly enough to take them out again. I told you I forgave you, so don't cry any more. . . ."

Don't keep holding on to your guilt. If you have confessed your sins to Christ, He has forgiven them and taken them away—forever.

May 6

Perfect in Weakness

When I am weak, then I am strong.
2 Corinthians 12:10

God's idea of strength and man's idea of strength are opposite one another.

The Lord told Paul, "My strength is made perfect in weakness" (2 Cor. 12:9). Having learned this lesson, Paul could then say, "When I am weak, then I am strong" (2 Cor. 12:10). A paradox? Not really. Only when Paul admitted his own weakness and was willing to get out of the way, could God take over and work.

If we try to do God's will in our own strength, then we can take the credit for whatever gets accomplished. But that isn't God's way! When we let His strength work through us, then He alone will get the glory—and that is as it should be.

In the Old Testament God repeatedly told the leaders of Israel to reduce the size of their armies, or He announced in advance how their victory would be won. Why? So they would place their trust in Him and not in their own strength. As someone has said, "God's work, done in God's way, will never lack for God's provision."

May 7

LONGING FOR GOD

My soul thirsts for God, for the living God.
PSALM 42:2

These words of the Psalmist sound strange to most people today: "My soul thirsts for God, for the living God." In an age preoccupied with the things of this world, God seems almost irrelevant.

But the Psalmist had discovered what most people realize sooner or later (even if they refuse to admit it): The things of this world can never satisfy the longings of our souls.

Only God can meet our deepest yearnings. As St. Augustine said centuries ago, "You have made us for Yourself, O God, and our hearts are restless until they find their rest in You."

What crowds out a yearning for God in your life? Don't let anything—or anyone—come between you and God. Isaiah wrote, "Why do you spend money for what is not bread, and your wages for what does not satisfy?" (Isa. 55:2).

God wants you to know Him in a personal way, and He has made this possible through Jesus Christ. He loves you, and He will give you His peace.

May 8

LOUD AND CLEAR

The mystery ... now has been revealed to His saints.
COLOSSIANS 1:26

Radio was just coming of age when I was a boy. We would gather around a crude homemade set and twist the tuning dials. Often the only sound was the squeak and squawk of static. It wasn't very exciting, but we kept at it. We knew that somewhere out there was the unseen transmitter and if we established contact, we could hear a voice loud and clear.

Does God speak to us? Is He trying to reach us? Yes! The problem is not with Him, but with us. Like that crude radio, we aren't attuned to Him.

We could only know God in one way: If He revealed Himself to us. And that is what He has done. He revealed Himself in the world He created, and in a fuller way He revealed Himself in His written Word, the Bible. Centuries ago He spoke to the prophets and the apostles, and by the inspiration of the Holy Spirit they wrote down His Word for us.

God is trying to break through to us—but we must "tune in" to His Word. Are you listening?

May 9

God's Secret Agents

He will give His angels charge
of you to guard you in all your ways.
Psalm 91:11, rsv

A secret agent is one who seeks to protect his country, his king, or his president against evil forces that are opposed to the one he serves. The American Secret Service is charged with protecting the president of the United States. They do an excellent job, but even they will tell you that someone who is fiercely determined to assassinate the president could be successful.

God has His own secret agents—the angels. Unseen and unrecognized by the world, they never fail in their appointed tasks.

Much has been written recently about angels—often not based on the Bible but on popular legends. But angels are real, and God has commanded them to watch over us. Only in eternity will we know how many accidents they prevented, or how often they kept Satan's malicious spirits at bay. In the meantime, we can take comfort in their presence, and thank God for the love He expresses for us through their service.

May 10

IN THE PRESENCE OF CHRIST

The upright shall dwell in your presence.
PSALM 140:13

What would you do if you were about to meet the Queen of England? I'm sure you would go out of your way to dress correctly and to be properly briefed so you didn't say the wrong thing or act in an improper way.

Someday you and I will meet a far greater Sovereign: The King of the universe. His dazzling glory far exceeds that of any earthly monarch, and in His presence we can only bow in humble worship and praise. Our cry will be that of Revelation: "You are worthy, O Lord, to receive glory and honor and power" (Rev. 4:11).

Are you prepared for that day when you will meet the King of kings face to face? No one knows the day or the hour when life will end. The time for you to prepare is now, by committing your life to Christ and beginning to live as a child of the King.

May 11

A STEP IN THE PROCESS

Blessed is the man whom You instruct, O Lord.
PSALM 94:12

A child develops muscles through exercise. Only when our muscles encounter resistance, do they become stronger.

In the same way, the Bible tells us that we only become stronger spiritually through exercise—through using our spiritual "muscles" to meet the challenges of life. This is especially true when we face suffering and affliction, for they are one of God's ways to make us strong. One reason God allows suffering to come to His people, the Bible says, is to discipline, chasten, and mold us.

In the last essay he wrote before he died, the great Christian writer C. S. Lewis said, "We have no right to happiness; only an obligation to do our duty." Sometimes our God-given duty will include suffering. When it does, ask God to teach you through it. Remember the Psalmist's words I quoted above: "Blessed is the man whom You instruct, O LORD."

May 12

A NEW CREATION

If anyone is in Christ, there is a new creation;
everything old has passed away.

2 CORINTHIANS 5:17, NRSV

I once heard a carpenter say that it is always better, and usually more economical, to construct a new house than to patch up an old one. This is even more true in the spiritual realm.

The old nature with its deceitfulness, its depravity, and its wickedness must give way to a new nature. And this is exactly what God stands ready to do. God says, "I will give you a new heart and put a new spirit within you" (Ezek. 36:26).

What a challenge! It is much more difficult to change our dispositions than it is our apparel. As a matter of fact, it is utterly impossible for us to change our dispositions in our own strength.

But God can! "If anyone is in Christ, there is a new creation." God doesn't just want to patch us up. He wants to remake us completely into the likeness of Christ! He wants to come into our lives and begin to change us from within. Have you asked Him to do that? He will!

May 13

Ambassadors Under Authority

*We are ambassadors for Christ, as though
God were pleading through us.*
2 Corinthians 5:20

What is an ambassador? He is a representative and servant of his government in a foreign land. He is not free to set his own policies or develop his own message, but must carry out the will of the government he represents. In other words, he is a person under authority.

In the same way we are called to live under the authority of Jesus Christ and the authority of the Scriptures. We are servants. We must live under the authority of the Word of God. We are called not to do our will, but Christ's.

The world today is looking for holy men and women who live under the authority of the Word of God. Unbelievers will not listen to what we say unless we back it up with the way we live. Are you a faithful ambassador for Christ to those around you?

LIVING A PEACEABLE LIFE

*Lead a quiet and peaceable life
in all godliness and reverence.*
1 TIMOTHY 2:2

As Christians we aren't to isolate ourselves from the world in which we live. We are part of society, and we share in its difficulties, problems, and hopes.

The Bible has much to say about our social responsibility. The Old Testament prophets condemned those who ignored the poor and exploited the weak. Not that it is easy. As Christians, we know human society is affected by sin, and any effort to improve society will always be incomplete and imperfect. We will never build a Utopia on earth.

But we must do all we can to alleviate suffering, and to strike at the root causes of injustice, racial prejudice, hunger, and violence. We are to work for a peaceable life and human dignity for others. Why? Because God loves this suffering world. Jesus saw the crowds and "was moved with compassion" (Matt. 9:36).

Christ is concerned about the whole person— including the society in which that person lives. Do we share His concern?

May 15

A GREAT GIFT

*The kingdom of God is ... righteousness
and peace and joy in the Holy Spirit.*
ROMANS 14:17

To the great gift of forgiveness God adds the great gift of the Holy Spirit. He is the source of power who meets our need to escape from the miserable weakness that grips us. He gives us the power to be truly good, as we yield ourselves to Him.

If we are to live a life of sanity in our modern world, if we wish to be men and women who can live victoriously, we need the two-sided gift God has offered us. First, the work of the Son of God *for* us; second, the work of the Spirit of God *in* us. In this way God has answered humanity's two great cries: the cry for forgiveness and the cry for goodness.

As a friend of mine has said, "I need Jesus Christ for my eternal life, and the Holy Spirit of God for my internal life." He might have added, " . . . so I can live my external life to the fullest."

GOD'S WORK

*As many as are led by the Spirit of
God, these are sons of God.*
ROMANS 8:14

The first key for usefulness in God's Kingdom
is humility. Pride cuts us off from God (and
from other people), and deceives us into
thinking we can do God's work without God's power.
When we rely on the Holy Spirit, however, He
sanctifies us and empowers us so we can be effective
tools in God's hands.

But there is a second key, and that is faith—faith
that God is sovereign, and that He is at work, even
if we can't see it. Habakkuk complained to God that
evil people were winning the day. But God replied, "I
will work a work in your days which you would not
believe, though it were told you" (Hab. 1:5).

God is at work, even in the midst of the problems,
pessimism, and frustrations of our day. He alone is
sovereign—and that is why we can trust Him, even
when the way seems dark.

May 17

CONFIDENCE AND PEACE

You will keep him in perfect peace,
whose mind is stayed on You.
ISAIAH 26:3

Peace carries with it the idea of unity, completeness, rest, ease, and security. Many times when I meet Jewish friends I greet them with *"Shalom,"* the Hebrew word for peace. And often, when I greet my Arab friends I use a similar term that they use for peace, *"Salam."*

Notice the key phrase in that verse: "whose mind is stayed on You." When troubles hit, our minds naturally focus on them. When suffering comes, all we can think about is the pain. It takes a deliberate act of the will to turn away from the problem and focus our minds on God.

When our minds are stayed on God, we won't be worried about the future, because we know it is in His hands. We won't tremble over what might happen, because our lives are built upon the solid rock of Christ.

When you and I yield to worry, we deny our Guide the right to lead us forward in confidence and peace. Don't cause Him to grieve over you by indulging in worry, but trust everything into His all-loving care.

May 18

WITNESS TO THE WORLD

*Rejoice with those who rejoice,
and weep with those who weep.*
ROMANS 12:15

J esus ate with publicans and sinners. Nearly everyone He associated with was an outcast. But His relationship with them was not purely social; it was redemptive.

We must not get our worlds mixed up at this point. God meant that we are not to mingle with the world and be polluted by the world, but we are to witness to the world. We are to "weep with those who weep," suffer with those who suffer, and identify ourselves with the poor, the sick, and the needy in body, mind, and spirit. How else can we reach them for Christ?

We are to love those who are involved in the world without being contaminated, influenced, or swayed by them. We achieve this distinction only by a close walk with Christ. Like Him, we are to be in the world, but not of the world.

It is good for a ship to be in the sea, but bad when the sea gets into the ship.

May 19

DISCOVER GOD'S GRACE

We conducted ourselves in the world ...
by the grace of God.
2 CORINTHIANS 1:12

I s God's grace really sufficient in times of trouble?
Can it sustain us in the midst of life's storms?
Yes—but to be honest, sometimes it's hard
for us to rely on God's grace instead of ourselves.
We think we have to grab control of our lives, and
believe the responsibility for shaping our future must
be in our hands.

When troubles come, therefore, we resist them
instead of depending on God to see us through.
Alexander Maclaren, the distinguished British
preacher of another generation, once wrote, "What
disturbs us in this world is not trouble, but our
opposition to trouble."

Put God to the test when troubles come. He won't
let you down. In the midst of a painful illness Paul
begged God to intervene and take it away. But God
replied, "My grace is sufficient for you" (2 Cor. 12:9).
It was for Paul, and it will be for you.

May 20

A HOME IN HEAVEN

If I go and prepare a place for you,
I will come again and receive you to Myself.
JOHN 14:3

During Christ's ministry on earth He had no permanent home. He once said, "Foxes have holes and birds of the air have nests, but the Son of Man has no place to lay his head" (Matt. 8:20, NIV).

What a contrast to the home He left in order to come to earth—His Heavenly home. From all eternity His dwelling place had been filled with unimaginable glory and splendor. And yet, the Bible says, He "emptied Himself . . . being born in human likeness" (Phil. 2:7, NRSV). Out of love for you and me, He left Heaven's glory for earth's misery.

But the story doesn't end there. Now He has returned to Heaven—and someday we will join Him. Think of it. He wants to share Heaven's glory with us!

One evening a little girl was taking a walk with her father. Looking up at the stars she exclaimed, "Daddy, if the wrong side of Heaven is so beautiful, what must the right side be like!"

May 21

THE GREATEST SECURITY

He who dwells in the secret place of the Most High shall abide under the shadow of the Almighty.
PSALM 91:1

Someone has said that the only certainty in life is uncertainty—and it is true. Governments collapse, stock markets plummet, wars destroy, disasters strike, relationships end. As the writer of Hebrews put it, "Here we have no continuing city" (Heb. 13:14).

Yet deep in the human heart is a yearning for security—a yearning that will not go away. We know we need a solid foundation to life, a foundation that cannot be shaken. Where will it be found?

Only God never changes. His love does not change, and neither do His promises. That is why we can look to Him for the security and stability we all seek. King David knew the secret: "He who dwells in the secret place of the Most High shall abide under the shadow of the Almighty."

Salvation is not an occasional, vague feeling of God's presence. It is actually dwelling with God, secure in His presence forever. Is *your* security in Christ?

In Giving, We Receive

Love one another as I have loved you.
JOHN 15:12

St. Francis of Assisi had discovered the secret of happiness when he prayed:

O Divine Master, grant that I may not
        so much seek
To be consoled as to console,
To be understood as to understand,
To be loved as to love;
For it is in giving that we receive;
It is in pardoning that we are pardoned;
It is in dying that we are born to eternal life!

Tears shed for self are tears of weakness, but tears of love shed for others are a sign of strength. I am not as sensitive as I ought to be until I am able to "weep o'er the erring one and lift up the fallen." And until I have learned the value of compassionately sharing others' sorrow, distress, and misfortune, I cannot know real happiness.

The opposite of love isn't hate. It's selfishness. Will you ask the Holy Spirit to free your life from selfishness and fill you instead with His love?

May 23

A POSITIVE INFLUENCE

Do not be conformed to this world,
but be transformed.
ROMANS 12:2

I have found that the casual Christian has little or no influence for good upon others. Only the Christian who refuses to compromise in matters of honesty, integrity, and morality is bearing an effective witness for Christ.

The casual, worldly Christian is prepared to do as the world does and will condone practices that are dishonest and unethical because he is afraid of the world's displeasure. He ignores the Bible's clear command: "Do not be conformed to this world."

Only by a life of obedience to the voice of the Spirit, by a daily dying to self, by a full dedication to Christ and constant fellowship with Him are we enabled to live a godly life and have a positive influence on this present ungodly world. Is the world changing you . . . or are you changing the world?

May 24

CHOOSE LIFE

I have set before you life and death;
... therefore choose life.

DEUTERONOMY 30:19

If God were to remove all evil from our world (but somehow leave human beings on the planet), it would mean that the essence of "humanness" would be destroyed. We would become robots.

Let me explain what I mean by this. If God eliminated evil by programming us to perform only good acts, we would lose this distinguishing mark— the ability to make choices. We would no longer be free moral agents. We would be reduced to the status of robots.

Let's take this a step further. Robots do not love. God created us with the capacity to love. Love is based upon one's right to choose to love. We cannot force others to love us. We can make them serve us or obey us. But true love is founded upon one's freedom to choose to respond.

Given the choice, I would rather be responsible for my actions than be a robot without responsibility! Are you using your ability to make decisions wisely—and using it for God?

May 25

VICTORY OVER SIN

*In all these things we are more than
conquerors through Him who loved us.*
ROMANS 8:37

We sing "Onward Christian soldiers, marching as to war," but so often when Satan mounts an attack against us we behave as if we were prisoners of war, or worse, conscientious objectors! But as Christians, we don't have to live defeated lives. God wants us to live victorious lives—lives that are constantly conquering sin.

There is only one way to have victory over sin. That is to walk so closely with Christ that sin no longer dominates your life. It becomes the exception rather than the rule.

Why does a close walk with Christ make the difference? Simply this: The closer we are to Christ, the farther we are from Satan. The Bible says, "Resist the devil and he will flee from you. Draw near to God and He will draw near to you" (James 4:7–8). Is the devil farther away from you today than he was a week ago? If not, why?

May 26

Relinquish Control

This is God, our God forever and ever;
He will be our guide even to death.

Psalm 48:14

The story is told of a little girl whose father was an airline pilot. As they crossed the Atlantic, a storm came up. The flight attendant awakened the little girl and told her to fasten her seat belt because they were in some turbulent weather. The little girl opened her eyes, saw the lightning flashing around the plane, and asked, "Is Daddy at the controls?" The flight attendant replied, "Yes, your father is in the cockpit." The little girl smiled, closed her eyes, and went back to sleep.

God is at the controls of our lives. Or, rather, He wants to be at the controls. But He gives us the freedom to pilot ourselves as we wish. The problem is that we often crack up, much as we could expect to do if we took the controls of an airplane we had not been taught to fly.

God knows us. He knows our strengths and weaknesses, and He knows what is best for us. If we will only relinquish the control of our lives to Him, He will see us safely home.

May 27

DEFLECT DESPAIR

*[God] gives us the victory through
our Lord Jesus Christ.*
1 CORINTHIANS 15:57, NIV

There is a story about Martin Luther going through a period of discouragement and depression. For days his long face graced the family table and dampened the family's home life. One day his wife came to the breakfast table all dressed in black, as if she were going to a funeral service. When Martin asked her who had died, she replied, "Martin, the way you've been behaving lately, I thought God had died, so I came prepared to attend His funeral."

Her gentle but effective rebuke drove straight to Luther's heart, and as a result the great Reformer resolved never again to allow worldly care, resentment, depression, discouragement, or frustration to defeat him. By God's grace, he vowed, he would submit his life to the Savior and reflect His grace in a spirit of rejoicing, whatever came.

When was the last time you praised God in the midst of despair? Don't wait until you "feel like it," or you'll never do it. Do it, and then you'll feel like it!

May 28

ONE WAY

*I am the way, the truth, and the life. No one
comes to the Father except through Me.*
JOHN 14:6

An old saying declares: "All roads lead to
Rome." Perhaps it was true in the ancient
world—but today, you can get lost anywhere!
The road you are on may lead in exactly the opposite
direction from your goal. The only sure way to reach
your destination is to consult a good road map or ask
someone who knows the way.

Not all roads lead to God, as some suggest. The
reason? There is a roadblock that keeps man from
reaching God—the roadblock of sin. But God has
provided a map—the Bible—and He has provided
us with One who knows the way and can give us
directions—Jesus Christ.

Jesus did *not* say, "I am one of many roads to
God." What He said was, "I am *the* way." That wasn't
arrogance, or narrow-mindedness, or lack of
compassion. It was truth—because only Christ came
from Heaven to pay the price for our sins. Follow
Christ and never be lost!

May 29

FROM TRIAL TO TRIUMPH

Walk in wisdom ... redeeming the time.
COLOSSIANS 4:5

The master musician knows that suffering precedes glory and acclaim. He knows the hours, days, and months of grueling practice and self-sacrifice that precede the one hour of perfect rendition when his efforts are applauded.

The master craftsman knows that years of work, sacrifice, and suffering as an apprentice precede his being promoted to the master of his trade.

The student knows that years of study, self-denial, and commitment precede the triumphant day of graduation with honors.

Astronauts spend years training for a flight that can be as short as a few days.

The Bible teaches that sacrifice and discipline are necessary if we are to be faithful servants of Christ. Paul wrote, "I discipline my body and bring it into subjection, lest, when I have preached to others, I myself should become disqualified" (1 Cor. 9:27).

Discipline your time ... discipline your eyes ... discipline your mind ... discipline your body ... all for the sake of Christ.

May 30

HOPE FOR THE HOME

*He sets the poor on high, . . . and
makes their families like a flock.*
PSALM 107:41

One of the primary reasons for the breakdown in the home is that we have forgotten God's commands about marriage.

God gave marriage to us, and His standards have not changed. Jesus said, "A man shall leave his father and mother and be joined to his wife. . . . Therefore what God has joined together, let not man separate" (Matt. 19:5-6).

Divorce was not part of God's original design—nor is it now. The Bible declares, "The LORD God of Israel says that He hates divorce" (Mal. 2:16). Marriage is a symbol of the unity between Christ and His church—a unity that should never be torn.

No marriage is beyond repair with God's help. But we must humble ourselves and put aside our pride and self-will. We must put others ahead of ourselves.

If divorce has happened to you, God can forgive the past, heal the present, and give hope for the future. But if you are married, treasure your spouse as a gift from God, and yield your marriage to Christ.

May 31

JESUS WILL ANSWER

He will give His angels charge of you
to guard you in all your ways.
PSALM 91:11, RSV

Once a poor Chinese woman went up to the foothills to cut grass. Her baby was tied to her back and a little child walked beside her. Just as she reached the top of a hill, she heard a roar. Frightened, she turned and saw a mother tigress springing at her, followed by her two cubs.

The illiterate Chinese woman had never attended school or church, but a missionary once told her about Jesus, "who is able to help you when you are in trouble." As the tiger's claws tore into her arm, the woman cried out, "O Jesus, help me!" The tiger, instead of attacking again, suddenly turned and ran away.

What "beasts" are attacking you? Chances are you will never be attacked by a wild tiger, but you will be attacked by doubts, fears, worry, loneliness, or despair.

Cry out to Jesus and He will answer you just as surely as the Chinese woman's desperate cry was heard and answered.

June

Pray that God will open your eyes to needs you can help meet in the lives of people you know.

June 1

His Most Precious Blood

Jesus Christ ... loved us and washed us
from our sins in His own blood.
Revelation 1:5

When J. P. Morgan, the multimillionaire, died, it was found that his will consisted of about 10,000 words and 37 articles. He made many transactions, some involving large sums of money.

But we are left in no doubt as to what he considered his most important transaction: "I commit my soul into the hands of my Savior, in full confidence that, having redeemed and washed it in His most precious blood, He will present it faultless before my heavenly Father; and I entreat my children to maintain and defend, at all hazard and at any cost of personal sacrifice, the blessed doctrine of the complete atonement for sin through the blood of Jesus Christ, once offered, and through that alone."

In the matter of his soul's eternal blessing, J. P. Morgan's vast wealth was powerless. He was just as dependent on God's mercy as was the dying thief at Calvary. No matter who you are or what you have done, only Christ can save you, for only "the blood of Jesus Christ ... cleanses ... from all sin" (1 John 1:7).

June 2

ASK AND RECEIVE

*Whatever things you ask when you pray, believe that
you receive them, and you will have them.*

MARK 11:24

Someone has said that before our prayers can
mean anything to God, they must first mean
something to us. Mindlessly repeating a prayer
we memorized in childhood, or vaguely asking God to
bless everyone, everywhere—that isn't authentic prayer.
Prayer is speaking to God about the deepest concerns
of our hearts.

What is the source of true prayer? It is a heart
attuned to God. It is a life lived in loving obedience
to the Father. The Bible says, "And whatever we
ask we receive from Him, because we keep His
commandments and do those things that are
pleasing in His sight" (1 John 3:22).

God delights in the prayers of His children—
prayers that express our love for Him, prayers that
share our deepest burdens with Him. Don't pray
casually or thoughtlessly, but "come boldly to the
throne of grace, that [you] may obtain mercy and
find grace to help in time of need" (Heb. 4:16).

June 3

LIVING A HOLY LIFE

Lay up for yourselves
treasures in heaven.
MATTHEW 6:20

An old man, a great man of God, lay on his deathbed. He summoned his grandson to come to his side. Calling the boy's name, he said, "I don't know what type of work I will be doing in Heaven, but if it's allowed, I'm going to ask the Lord Jesus to let me help build your mansion. You be sure you send up plenty of the right materials."

Living a life of purity and love, leading others to Christ as we share our faith, doing good works in Christ's name—all of these things are materials that may be sent on ahead. These can never be touched by the fluctuations in the earthly economy, by natural disaster, or by thievery.

What kind of materials are you sending up to Heaven?

REST FOR THE WEARY

Come to Me . . . and I will give you rest.
MATTHEW 11:28

We forget that Jesus was human as well as divine. He had calluses on His hands. If the chisel slipped and cut His finger, His blood was red and warm like ours. He knew what it meant to work long hours, to come in at night tired and weary.

That is one of the reasons Jesus could say with such appeal, "Come to Me, all you who labor and are heavy laden, and I will give you rest" (Matt. 11:28). When we are exhausted and hurting, we can take comfort from the fact that Jesus knows what it is to be exhausted and hurting also.

But the greatest work Jesus did was not in the carpenter's shop, nor at the marriage feast in Cana where He turned the water into wine. The greatest work Jesus did was not when He made the blind to see, the deaf to hear, the dumb to speak, nor even the dead to rise.

What was His greatest work?

His greatest work was what He accomplished through the Cross and Resurrection. There the burden of our sins was placed on Him, and there He won our salvation. And that is why we can come by faith to Him, and He will give us rest.

June 5

MORE ATTACHED TO GOD

God is our refuge and strength,
an ever-present help in trouble.
PSALM 46:1, NIV

A young Irishman, Joseph Scriven (1820–1886), was deeply in love with a young woman, and their marriage plans had been made. The night before their wedding, however, she drowned in a tragic accident. For months Scriven was bitter, in utter despair.

At last he turned to Christ, and through His grace, found peace and comfort. Out of this experience he wrote the familiar hymn that has brought consolation to millions of aching hearts: "What a friend we have in Jesus / All our sins and griefs to bear!"

Sometimes our way lies in the sunlight. It was so for Joseph Scriven as he approached his wedding day. But like him, we may find that our path also leads through the dark shadows of loss, disappointment, and sorrow.

Yet even sorrows turn to blessings when they make us less attached to the earth and more attached to God. Then more than ever we discover that Jesus truly is our friend—"All our sins and griefs to bear!"

June 6

TAKE THE LEAP

By my God I can leap over a wall.
PSALM 18:29

The Bible confronts us with our moral independence within ourselves and our spiritual dependence upon God.

In the picturesque words of the Psalm, David says, "By my God I can leap over a wall." We can jump over some barriers in life by our own will and our own efforts; God has not left us completely powerless. But some walls are so high we need more than this.

The Psalmist knew such walls. They could be leaped only with the help of God. When we try to jump over them by ourselves, we repeatedly fall short. But with God's help, we can conquer them.

What walls do you need to conquer? A habit you cannot break? An emotion that defeats you? An attitude that separates you from others? A heart beset with doubt or discouragement or fear? Whatever it is, with God's help you can leap over that wall.

June 7

THE SEAL OF THE SPIRIT

When you believed, you were marked in him
with a seal, the promised Holy Spirit.
EPHESIANS 1:13, NIV

God places a seal on us when we receive Christ. And that seal is a person—the Holy Spirit. By the Spirit's presence God gives us security and establishes His ownership over us.

The Spirit is also God's pledge. He not only seals the arrangement, but He represents God's commitment to see us through. And fellowship with the Spirit is a sample of what we can expect when we come into our inheritance in Heaven.

Finally, the Spirit witnesses to us, by the Scriptures and within our hearts, that Christ died for us, and by faith in Him we have become God's children.

What a wonderful thing to know the Holy Spirit has been given to us as a seal—a pledge—and a witness! May each of these give us new assurance of God's unchanging love for us, and give us confidence as we seek to live for Him.

A CLEAR CONSCIENCE

I myself always strive to have a conscience
without offense toward God and men.
ACTS 24:16

Benjamin Franklin composed this little rhyme:
"Keep conscience clear, then never fear."
George Bernard Shaw, the great Irish writer
said, "Better keep yourself clean and bright; you are
the window through which you must see the world."

If conscience was such a vital concept to these
secular writers, how much more concerned should we
as Christians be that our consciences are
"without offense toward God and men"? Without
conscience we would be like rudderless ships at sea, or
missiles without a guidance system.

God has given our conscience to us. Its very
presence is a reflection of God in the human soul.
Sin, however, can dull or even distort our conscience,
silencing its voice and leading us astray. But God's
Word can purify and sharpen our conscience—and
when that happens, "He leads [us] in paths of
righteousness for His name's sake" (Ps. 23:3).

Is this happening in your life?

June 9

IN THE TIME OF TROUBLE

Cast your burden on the Lord,
and He shall sustain you.
PSALM 55:22

Years ago I came across this oft-quoted prayer: "God grant me the serenity to accept things I cannot change, the courage to change the things I can, and wisdom to know the difference." This prayer expresses an important thought; one we should all pray—and live.

Some things in life cannot be changed—and some can. Some things God has given to us as fixed realities that we must accept. And some things He would have us not accept, but (with His help) work to change. If we fail to do both of these—to accept some things and work to change others—we will end up burdened with worry, undeserved guilt, and frustration.

Someone once said, "Worry is the interest paid on trouble before it comes due." Instead, God would have us learn to trust Him. "Cast your burden on the LORD, and He shall sustain you."

GOD'S GOOD PROMISE

*Blessed be the Lord.... There has not failed
one word of all His good promise.*

1 KINGS 8:56

When we purchase something of great value—a house, for example—we are usually required to put down a deposit to indicate our sincerity and to promise that our intentions are serious. That deposit is a form of insurance, a guarantee that adds substance to our word.

God has made some incredible promises to us—promises that stagger our imaginations. He has promised that we might have a relationship with Him through His Son. He has promised never to leave us or forsake us and to be with us always. He has promised to take us to Heaven when we die. The Bible is full of God's promises.

Someone might ask, "What insurance do we have that God is serious? How do we know His promises can be trusted?" God's deposit is the most precious investment anyone could make: His Son, who by His death and resurrection purchased our salvation—completely and fully. Not only is Jesus Christ a sufficient "down payment" on God's promises, He is, in fact, payment in full!

June 11

THE PRIVILEGE OF PRAYER

Ask, and you will receive, that your joy may be full.
JOHN 16:24

What a privilege is ours: the privilege of prayer!

Just think of it: You and I have the incredible privilege of approaching the God of the Universe, "the High and Lofty One who inhabits eternity, whose name is Holy" (Isa. 57:15)! We can only do this because Jesus Christ has opened the way.

We are to pray in times of adversity, lest we become faithless and unbelieving.

We are to pray in times of prosperity, lest we become boastful and proud.

We are to pray in times of danger, lest we become fearful and doubting.

We are to pray in times of security, lest we become self-sufficient.

Pray, believing, in the promise of God's Word that "If we ask anything according to His will, He hears us" (1 John 5:14).

June 12

Overflowing Joy

But the fruit of the Spirit is . . . joy.
GALATIANS 5:22

The word *joy* has all but disappeared from our current Christian vocabulary. One reason is because we have confused joy with happiness, and have come to believe it is found in pleasure, security, and prosperity. In doing this, however, we have believed a lie that Satan is constantly telling the world to believe.

But James did not say, "Count it all joy when you fall into an easy chair." He said, "Count it all joy when you fall into various trials" (James 1:2).

Joy is not the same as happiness—although they may overlap. Happiness depends on circumstances; joy depends on God. Happiness vanishes when life turns painful; joy keeps going and may even grow.

Joy comes from a living, vital relationship with God. It comes from knowing this world is only temporary, and someday we will be with God forever. It comes from the fact that although we do not yet see God, we "believe in him and are filled with an inexpressible and glorious joy" (1 Pet. 1:8, NIV). It comes from a life of submission to the Holy Spirit—regardless of circumstances.

June 13

A BEACON OF HOPE

If I go and prepare a place for you, I will come again....
JOHN 14:3

The late C. S. Lewis in his remarkable book *Christian Behavior*, said, "Hope is one of the theological virtues." He meant that a continual looking forward to the eternal world is not, as some people think, a form of escapism or wishful thinking, but one of the things a Christian is meant to do.

This does not mean we are to leave the present world as it is. If you read history you will find that the Christians who did the most for the present world were those who thought the most of the next. It is only since Christians have largely ceased to think of the next world that they have become so ineffective in this one. "Aim at heaven," said Lewis, "and you will get earth thrown in. Aim at earth, and you will get neither."

In the midst of the pessimism, gloom, and frustration of the present hour there is one bright beacon of hope—and that is the promise of Jesus Christ, "If I go and prepare a place for you, I will come again and receive you to Myself" (John 14:3).

POWER FOR PROBLEMS

I can do all things through
Christ who strengthens me.
PHILIPPIANS 4:13

A friend told me of a non-believer who came to him in the midst of a troubled day. Knowing my friend was a Christian, the man asked, "If I get born again, will all of my problems go away?"

"No," said my friend, "but you will have the power to deal with them."

God will give us wisdom and courage. He will surround us with brothers and sisters in Christ to help carry our burdens, and even provide us with insight and practical assistance.

Satan will always try to discourage those who belong to Christ. When problems persist, he may even whisper, "See, God doesn't care about you!" But with the Holy Spirit's help, we can combat the evil one and contradict his lies.

If God dismissed all our problems with a single stroke, we would be left defenseless, unequipped to meet the inevitable attacks of the enemy of our souls. But in the midst of life's problems God supplies everything we need to see us through.

June 15

ACCEPT GOD'S FREEDOM

Draw near to God and He will draw near to you.
JAMES 4:8

One day a little child was playing with a valuable vase. He put his hand into it and could not take it out. His father, too, tried his best to get the little boy's hand out, but all in vain. They were thinking of breaking the vase when the father said, "Now, my son, make one more try. Open your hand and hold your fingers out straight as you see me doing and then pull."

To the father's astonishment the little fellow said, "Oh no, Daddy. I couldn't put my fingers out like that because if I did I would drop my penny."

Smile if you will—but thousands of us are like that little boy, so busy holding on to the world's worthless trifles that we cannot accept God's freedom.

What "trifle" is keeping you from God? A sin you won't let go of? An unworthy goal you are determined to reach? A dishonorable relationship you won't give up? I beg you to drop that trifle in your heart. Surrender! Let go and let God have His way in your life.

NEARER THAN YOU THINK

His angels ... keep you in all your ways.
PSALM 91:11

Occasionally I see reports of happenings that cannot be humanly explained—of visitors unexpectedly appearing to assist in times of crisis, or warning of impending danger. These can only be explained as the intervention of God's angels.

In the Bible, angels occasionally assumed visible form—at the birth of Jesus, for example. But usually angels go about their business unseen and unrecognized. They never draw attention to themselves, but point us instead to Christ.

C. S. Lewis once said that we tend to make one of two errors about Satan: We either make too little of him, or we make too much.

The same could be said of angels. Don't make too little of them. God has given "His angels charge over you, to keep you in all your ways" (Ps. 91:11). On the other hand, don't worship them or become preoccupied with them. Instead, thank God for His angels and rejoice in their unseen watchfulness over you.

June 17

GOD'S TRUE PURPOSES

Whatever you ask in My name, that I will do....
JOHN 14:13

Prayer links us with God's true purposes, for us and for the world. It not only brings the blessings of God's will to our own personal lives, it brings us the added blessing of being in step with God's plan.

Prayer also—in ways we will never fully understand this side of eternity—makes us partners with God in what He is doing in the world. God works through our prayers!

The model prayer Jesus has given us concludes with, "Thine is the kingdom, and the power, and the glory for ever" (Matt. 6:13, KJV). Remember, too, that we must seek God's glory in our prayers and not just our own selfish desires. If we are to have our prayers answered, we must be willing to give God the glory when He acts—no matter what the result. Our Lord said to His disciples, "Whatever you ask in My name, that I will do, that the Father may be glorified in the Son" (John 14:13).

June 18

WHITE AS SNOW

Wash me, and I shall be whiter than snow.

Snow is so white that one can see almost anything that is dropped on it, even at great distances. We can take the whitest object we can find, like newly washed clothing, but when we place it next to snow it still looks dirty by comparison.

Our lives are like that. At times, we may think of ourselves as morally good and decent; we are content that "we are not like other men." But compared to God's purity, we are defiled and filthy.

In spite of our sins and uncleanness, God still loves us. And because He loves us, He decided to provide for us a purity we could never attain on our own. That is why He gave His Son, Jesus Christ, to die for us on the Cross. Only when our sins have been washed in the blood of Jesus Christ will we appear as white as snow in the eyes of God. Thank God today that you are now "whiter than snow," because "you were washed . . . in the name of the Lord Jesus and by the Spirit of our God" (1 Cor. 6:11)!

June 19

SINCERE DEVOTION

The fruit of the Spirit is love,
joy, peace, . . . gentleness, self-control.
GALATIANS 5:22–23

We should seek to produce the fruit of the Spirit in our lives. Or to put it more accurately, we should allow the Holy Spirit to produce His fruit in our lives.

You say, "I am powerless to produce such fruit. You don't know how weak and self-centered I am. It would be utterly impossible for me to do so!"

With that I agree! That is, we can't produce this fruit in our own strength. When the Spirit of God dwells in us and has control of our lives, He will produce that fruit. Our responsibility is to cultivate the soil of our hearts through sincere devotion and surrender, so He might find favorable ground to produce His fruit.

I might have a fruit tree in my yard, but if the soil isn't enriched and the bugs carefully destroyed, it will not yield a full crop. What keeps the Holy Spirit from producing His fruit in your life?

June 20

THE BREVITY OF LIFE

What is your life? You are a mist that appears
for a little while and then vanishes.

JAMES 4:14, NIV

S everal years ago a university student asked
me what had been my biggest surprise in life.
Immediately I replied, "The brevity of life."
Almost before we know it, the years have passed and
life is almost over.

On one hand, life's brevity should challenge us.
If ever we are to live for Christ and share Him with
others, it must be now. Jesus said, "The night is
coming when no one can work" (John 9:4).

But life's brevity should also comfort us. Life is
short—and before us is eternity! When sufferings
overwhelm us or difficulties assail us we know they
will soon be over. Paul wrote, "Our light affliction,
which is but for a moment, is working for us a far
more exceeding and eternal weight of glory.....
For the things which are seen are temporary"
(2 Cor. 4:17–18).

Don't live as if this life will continue forever. It
won't. Live instead with eternity in view!

June 21

FREE BUT NOT CHEAP

If anyone desires to come after Me,
let him ... take up his cross, and follow Me.
MATTHEW 16:24

During the early years of the twentieth century, Bill Borden turned his back on one of America's great family fortunes to become a missionary to China. He only got as far as Egypt where, still in his twenties, he died of typhoid fever. Before his death he wrote, "No reserves, no retreats, no regrets!"

Discipleship is always costly. No, it may not cost us our lives. But it will cost us. It will cost us our plans, our wills, our selfish desires. Jesus' standard has not changed: "If anyone desires to come after Me, let him deny himself and take up his cross, and follow Me" (Matt. 16:24). Instead of controlling our lives, we turn them over to Christ as Lord.

Someone has said, "Salvation is free but not cheap." It cost Jesus His life, and it will cost us as well. But could anything be greater? Could anything be more fulfilling?

Follow Christ, and at life's end you will be able to say, "No regrets!"

June 22

OUR OMNIPOTENT HELPER

*The Spirit of truth who proceeds from
the Father, He will testify of Me.*
JOHN 15:26

God the Holy Spirit is equal with the Son and
with the Father in every respect. Although
the doctrine of the Trinity is difficult for us
to understand, the Bible teaches that He is co-equal
with God the Father and co-equal with God the Son.

The Bible also teaches that the Holy Spirit is a
Person. He is never to be referred to as "it." He is
not an impersonal power or force, nor is He just a
divine influence or agent. He is a mighty Person, the
Holy Spirit of God.

The Bible tells us as well that He is omnipotent.
That means He has all power. It tells us also that He
is omnipresent. That means He is everywhere at the
same time.

What should this mean to me? With the
seventeenth-century Anglican bishop, Jeremy Taylor,
I can say, "It is impossible for that man
to despair who remembers that his Helper
is omnipotent."

June 23

SUFFICIENT GRACE

My grace is sufficient for you.
2 CORINTHIANS 12:9

The prayer of Jesus in the Garden of Gethsemane is perhaps the greatest, most moving prayer ever uttered. In it our Lord asked that the cup of crucifixion, which was about to be thrust upon Him, might be taken away. But then, in the very next breath He said, "Nevertheless, not as I will, but as You will" (Matt. 26:39). What a prayer! What strength! What power!

When the apostle Paul asked God to remove his "thorn in the flesh," God did not remove it, saying instead, "My grace is sufficient for you" (2 Cor. 12:9). Rather than complain or become angry at God, Paul joyfully submitted to God's will. He discovered that God's grace truly was sufficient, even in the midst of pain.

Christ desires to be with you in whatever crisis you may find yourself. Call upon His name. See if He will not do as He promised He would. He may not make your problems go away, but He will give you the power to deal with them and to overcome them by His grace.

CHANGED FOR LIFE

We . . . are being transformed into
the same image from glory to glory.
2 CORINTHIANS 3:18

You can scrub a pig, sprinkle Chanel No. 5 on him, put a ribbon around his neck, and take him into your living room. But when you turn him loose, he will jump into the first mud puddle he sees because his nature has never been changed. He is still a pig.

We constantly try to reform ourselves. Stores are filled with self-help books claiming to hold the secret to personal reformation. But such efforts are only temporary at best. A deeper transformation is needed—a transformation of the heart.

And it is possible! The Bible teaches that when we come to Christ, we are spiritually born again. God's Spirit comes to live within us and change us. Our motives change, our objectives change, our dispositions change, our eternal destiny changes.

No, it doesn't happen all at once. We will spend the rest of our lives learning what it means to follow Christ. But it begins now, as we open our hearts to Him. Is your life "being transformed . . . from glory to glory"?

June 25

MAKING GOOD DECISIONS

Then the king ... rejected the advice of the elders.
2 CHRONICLES 10:13

T ragically, many people are the victims of their own bad decisions. Faced with choices every day, they turn their backs on what is right or what is best and decide instead on what is wrong or what will bring them harm. Only afterward do they realize that bad decisions always result in bad consequences.

King Rehoboam stubbornly rejected the wise advice of his nation's elders and instead followed those who told him only what he wanted to hear. As a result, conflict broke out and the nation divided. The Bible warns, "Whatever a man sows, that he will also reap" (Gal. 6:7).

Life is filled with decisions—some minor, but some life changing. How will you make them? The most important thing I can tell you is this: Seek God's will in *every* decision. Pray. Turn to the Scriptures. Seek the advice of godly friends. Ask the Holy Spirit to guide you. God loves you, and His way is *always* best.

WHAT GOD CALLS WISDOM

He Himself is our peace, who ... has broken
down the middle wall of separation.

EPHESIANS 2:14

Some time ago a university professor was quoted as saying, "There are two things that will never be solved—the problems of race and war." Perhaps he was right; only time will tell.

Admittedly, however, the Bible gives us little reason for optimism about any lasting solution to these problems. The reason? Both racism and war have their origin in the pride and covetousness of the human heart. Until our hearts are changed, we will fall back into the same destructive sins.

That doesn't mean we throw up our hands in despair and refuse to do anything about war or racism—not at all. The Bible calls Christ the "Prince of Peace" (Isa. 9:6). He shattered the prejudices of His day by reaching out to those of another race, and He expects no less of us.

The object of the Cross is not only pardon for our sins, it is also a changed life. Ask God to help you be an instrument of His love to those around you.

June 27

TRUST AND OBEY

Blessed is the one who trusts in the Lord.
PSALM 40:4, NIV

Some years ago someone gave my little boy a dollar. He brought it to me and said, "Daddy, keep this for me." But in a few minutes he came back and said, "Daddy, I'd better keep my own dollar." He tucked it in his pocket and went out to play. In a few minutes he came back with tears in his eyes, saying, "Daddy, I lost my dollar. Help me find it."

How often we commit our burdens to the Lord and then fail to trust Him by taking matters into our own hands. Then, when we have messed things up, we pray, "Oh, Lord, help me, I'm in trouble."

The choice is yours. Do you want to trust your life in God's "pocket" or keep it in your own? The Bible's promise is true: "Blessed is the one who trusts in the LORD."

THE TRANSFER IS COMPLETE

He made Him ... to be sin for us, that we might become the righteousness of God in Him.

2 CORINTHIANS 5:21

When we come to Christ, the Bible says He imparts His righteousness to us. Once we were sinners in God's eyes; now He sees us as righteous because of Christ.

How could this happen? In ourselves we aren't righteous. As the Bible says, "There is none righteous, no, not one" (Rom. 3:10). But when we accept Christ, the filthy rags of our sin are replaced by the glorious robe of Christ's righteousness. Our sins were transferred to Him—and His righteousness was transferred to us.

Did we deserve it? No. Did we earn it? No. It is all of grace—all because of God's undeserved favor toward us in Christ. We can never win God's favor by our deeds, no matter how good we are. Only Christ can save us. Thank God that you now stand before Him, clothed in the perfect righteousness of Christ!

June 29

PEACE, PERFECT PEACE

I will give you assured peace in this place.
JEREMIAH 14:13

"Worry," says Vance Havner, "is like sitting in a rocking chair. It will give you something to do, but it won't get you anywhere." Worry and anxiety have hounded the human race since the beginning of time, and modern man with all his innovations has not found the cure for the plague of worry.

What is the answer? Imagine in your mind a ferocious ocean storm beating against a rocky shore. The lightning flashes, the thunder roars, the waves lash the rocks. But then imagine that you see a crevice in the rocky cliff—and inside is a little bird, its head serenely tucked under its wing, fast asleep. It knows the rock will protect it, and thus it sleeps in peace.

God promised Moses, "I will put you in the cleft of the rock, and will cover you with My hand" (Exod. 33:22). That is God's promise to us. Christ is our Rock, and we are secure in His hands forever. The storm rages, but our hearts are at rest.

KEEP HEAVEN IN VIEW

We are afflicted in every way, but not crushed.
2 CORINTHIANS 4:8, NRSV

I have found in my travels that those who keep Heaven in view remain serene and cheerful in the darkest day. If the glories of Heaven were more real to us, if we lived less for material things and more for things eternal and spiritual, we would be less easily disturbed by this present life.

This is not escapism, as some would argue. If anything, a firm faith in the future should make us more responsible in the present. All around us are people who never give a moment's thought to Heaven or eternity. How will they learn of the future if we don't tell them in the present? The real escapism, I would contend, is refusing to face the future that God has prepared for us.

In these days of darkness and upheaval and uncertainty, the trusting and forward-looking Christian remains optimistic and joyful, knowing that Christ someday must rule, and "if we endure, we shall also reign with Him" (2 Tim. 2:12).

July

*Pray that your friends, family,
co-workers, and neighbors will
recognize Christ's presence
and love in your life.*

July 1

A CLEAN SLATE

Create in me a clean heart, O God,
and renew a steadfast spirit within me.
PSALM 51:10

D id you ever have the experience in school of erasing an entire blackboard? When the slate has been wiped clean, it is as if nothing at all had ever been written on it.

This is what God does for us when we come to Him, confessing our sin and trusting Christ as our Savior and Lord. First John 1:9 says, "If we confess our sins, He is faithful and just to forgive us our sins, and to cleanse us from all unrighteousness." Note what He promises to do: forgive *and* cleanse. The slate is wiped clean! Only God can do that. We can't do it ourselves.

How many times in your life have you wished you could start all over again with a clean slate, with a new life? Resolve right now to allow God to wipe your slate clean by confessing your sins and letting Him give you a brand new start.

July 2

THE CALL OF CHRIST

The wisdom of this world is foolishness with God.
1 CORINTHIANS 3:19

Some may contend that the way for the Church to make the world a better place is to become like it. But whenever the Church does this, it ends up compromising its spiritual authority and losing its influence. Instead of changing the world, the world changes it.

God doesn't want us to isolate ourselves. In praying for His disciples Jesus said, "As You sent Me into the world, I also have sent them into the world" (John 17:18). If we isolate ourselves from others, we have no impact and demonstrate a lack of love.

But neither does God want us to become like the unbelieving world. We are to be separate, refusing to adopt its motives, attitudes, and patterns of behavior. The Bible warns, "All that is in the world—the lust of the flesh, the lust of the eyes, and the pride of life—is not of the Father but is of the world" (1 John 2:16). Let Christ fill your life, and there won't be room for the world.

July 3

THE LIGHT OF SALVATION

Whoever confesses that Jesus
is the Son of God, God abides in him.
1 JOHN 4:15

Only when we comprehend the great price God was willing to pay for our redemption do we begin to realize that something is horribly wrong with the human race. It must have a Savior, or it is doomed!

Sin cost God His very best. Is it any wonder the angels veiled their faces and were silent in their consternation as they witnessed the outworking of God's plan? How inconceivable it must have seemed to them, when they considered the fearful depravity of sin, that Jesus should shoulder it all.

But they were soon to unveil their faces and offer their praises again. A light was kindled that day at Calvary—"the light of the gospel of the glory of Christ, who is the image of God" (2 Cor. 4:4). The cross blazed with the glory of God as the most terrible darkness was shattered by the light of salvation. Satan's depraved legions were defeated; they could no longer keep humanity in darkness and defeat.

Has the light of the Gospel shone in your heart? And is it shining through you to others?

A STATUE OF LIBERTY

If the Son makes you free, you shall be free indeed.
JOHN 8:36

During the national observance of the one-hundredth anniversary of the Statue of Liberty in New York Harbor, I was struck by the great emphasis on the number of immigrants who had often left everything behind. Coming to America with nothing but the clothes on their backs, they risked their lives for something they valued more highly than everything they had left behind: freedom. They did not take their adopted country's hard-won freedom for granted—and neither must we.

Their experience is a picture of what we must do when we come to Christ. We must forsake our allegiance to this world, leave behind all that it offers, and become citizens of a new kingdom—the Kingdom of God. His statue of liberty is in the form of the Cross.

The statue in New York Harbor lifts her lamp "beside the golden door." The statue of liberty on that hill outside Jerusalem lights the way into eternal life.

July 5

THE KNOWLEDGE OF GOD

*Oh, the depth of the riches both of
the wisdom and knowledge of God!*
ROMANS 11:33

It was the mystery of lightning (so the story goes) that prompted Benjamin Franklin to attach a key to the tail of a kite during a thunderstorm, to prove the identity of lightning and electricity. We have always tried to understand the world around us; it is one of the things that sets us apart from the animals.

Some of the mysteries of the past have been fathomed by science. Others still puzzle us. This fact remains: All of the garnered wisdom of the ages is only a scratch on the surface of humanity's search for the knowledge of the universe.

This inability to comprehend fully the mysteries of God's creation does not in any way cast doubt on the Christian faith. On the contrary, it enhances our belief. We do not understand the intricate patterns of the stars in their courses, but we know that He who created them does, and that just as surely as He guides them, He is charting a safe course for us.

The next time you look into the heavens at night, remember the words of the Psalmist: "The heavens declare the glory of God" (Ps. 19:1).

July 6

A Glorious Grandstand

*Since we are surrounded by so great a cloud
of witnesses, let us lay aside every weight.*
HEBREWS 12:1

If the angels rejoice over one sinner who repents (Luke 15:10), then the angelic hosts are numbered among the spectators in the Heavenly grandstands. They are included among those who are referred to as "so great a cloud of witnesses" (Heb. 12:1); and they never miss any of the details of our earthly pilgrimage.

Nor does our God—Father, Son, and Holy Spirit—overlook what goes on here. As the Bible says, "All things are . . . open to the eyes of Him to whom we must give account" (Heb. 4:13).

In his book, *Though I Walk Through the Valley*, Dr. Vance Havner tells of an old preacher who worked into the night on a sermon for his small congregation. His wife inquired why he spent so much time on a message he would give to so few. To this the minister replied, "You forget, my dear, how large my audience will be!" Dr. Havner adds, "Nothing is trivial here if heaven looks on. We shall play a better game if, 'seeing we are encompassed,' we remember who is in the grandstand!"

July 7

THE DAY IS AT HAND

Put on the armor of light.
ROMANS 13:12, NASB

I once read about a sundial on which was inscribed the cryptic message, "It is later than you think." Travelers would often pause to meditate on the meaning of that phrase. Its author undoubtedly wanted to remind others of the shortness and uncertainty of life.

We Christians have a sundial—the Word of God. From Genesis to Revelation it bears its warning: "It is later than you think." Writing to the Christians of his day Paul said, "It is already the hour for you to awaken from sleep; for now salvation is nearer to us than when we believed. The night is almost gone, and the day is at hand. Let us therefore lay aside the deeds of darkness and put on the armor of light" (Rom. 13:11–12, NASB).

Learn to live each day as if it were your last. Someday it will be.

GOD FEELS WHAT WE FEEL

Through the Lord's mercies we are not consumed,
because His compassions fail not.

LAMENTATIONS 3:22

When I was a small boy, I thought of God as an old man with a long white beard. After all, hadn't Michaelangelo and other artists painted Him that way? Perhaps in my childish mind I thought He resembled an old man in other ways also—somewhat feeble and harmless, not quite in touch with me and my problems.

Later, as I read the Bible, I realized that God is a spirit. He does not have a body, nor is He confined to one place (as a physical being would be). At the same time, He has the attributes of a person: He thinks, He speaks, He communicates, He loves, He becomes angry, He grieves. Because God is a person, He feels what we feel.

No matter what we face, He understands what we are going through. He even understands our temptations, for Christ "has been tempted in every way, just as we are—yet he did not sin" (Heb. 4:15, NIV). And that is why you can bring anything—*anything*—to Him in prayer, confident that He will understand.

July 9

A Thirst for Righteousness

*Blessed are those who hunger
and thirst for righteousness.*
MATTHEW 5:6

God is the only source of true happiness, because He offers those intangibles that we mistakenly believe can be found on earth: contentment, security, peace, and hope for the future. None of these can be found in a job, a human relationship, money, power, or position. They are God's alone to give.

How hard it is for us to believe this, however! This is understandable if we haven't given our lives to Christ; then, the Bible says, our spiritual "eyes" are still blinded, unable to see God's truth until the Holy Spirit opens them. But it can happen to us as believers also—falling into the pattern of the world, vainly pursuing happiness in the same ways the world does.

That is why the Lord Jesus, in His Sermon on the Mount, told where ultimate happiness lies: "Blessed are those who hunger and thirst for righteousness, for they shall be *filled.*" This is God's promise—and it is true.

Riches . . . or righteousness? Which will be your goal?

July 10

PEACEMAKERS

*Blessed are the peacemakers for
they shall be called sons of God.*

MATTHEW 5:9

To have peace *with* God and to have the peace *of* God in our hearts is not enough. This vertical relationship must have a horizontal outworking, or our faith is in vain. Jesus said that we were to love the Lord with all our hearts and our neighbors as ourselves.

This dual love for God and others is like the positive and negative poles of a battery—unless both connections are made, we have no power. A personal faith is normally useless unless it has a social application. (A notable exception would seem to be the thief on the cross, who repented only moments before his death—and yet countless people have been touched over the centuries by his example of faith.)

If we have peace *with* God and the peace *of* God, we will become peacemakers. We will not only strive to be at peace with our neighbors, but we will be leading them to discover the source of true peace in Christ. Is the peace of Christ in your life overflowing to others?

July 11

I Am the Truth

You shall know the truth,
and the truth shall make you free.
JOHN 8:32

M any today say there is no such thing as absolute truth. From philosophers to pop musicians, the word goes out that "truth" is only what you want it to be, and what is "true" for you isn't necessarily "true" for anyone else.

But Jesus Christ is absolute truth. Dozens of times He declares, "I tell you the truth." In one of His boldest and most uncompromising statements He affirmed, "I am the way, the truth, and the life" (John 14:6). The writer of the Gospel of John stated, "Grace and truth came through Jesus Christ" (John 1:17). James said that God "chose to give us birth through the word of truth" (James 1:18, NIV).

Do not be misled by the moral and spiritual relativity of our age. God has revealed His truth to us—in His written Word, the Bible, and in the living Word, Jesus Christ. And because Jesus is absolute truth, you can depend on Him absolutely!

CRUCIFIED WITH CHRIST

Be imitators of God as dear children.
EPHESIANS 5:1

The story is told of a man who glanced at the obituary column in his local newspaper. To his surprise he saw his own name, indicating that he had just died. At first he laughed about it. But soon the telephone began to ring. Stunned friends and acquaintances called to inquire and to offer their sympathy.

Finally, in irritation, he called the newspaper editor and angrily reported that even though he had been reported dead in the obituary column he was very much alive. The editor was apologetic and embarrassed. Then in a flash of inspiration, he said, "Don't worry, sir, I'll make it all right; tomorrow I'll put your name in the births column."

This may sound like merely a humorous incident, but it is also a spiritual parable. Not until we have allowed our old selves to be nailed to the cross and to die, can our new selves be born again and emerge to grow up into the likeness of Christ. The Bible is marvelously true: "And you He made alive, who were dead in trespasses and sins. . . . Therefore be imitators of God as dear children" (Eph. 2:1; 5:1).

July 13

God Promises Protection

I will never leave you nor forsake you.
Hebrews 13:5

Never doubt that you are in the midst of a battle—a spiritual battle with Satan, who will do everything he can to discourage and defeat you. Never underestimate his determination or misunderstand his intentions.

God wants to teach us how to defend ourselves against sin and Satan. Satan, the ultimate bully, attacks us at our weakest points and wants to defeat us so that we will not be effective for God.

God offers spiritual "training" to build us up inside in much the same way that physical exercise can build us up on the outside. He has also provided all the resources we need to defend ourselves and keep Satan at bay. These include the Bible, prayer, faith, righteous living, and the Holy Spirit within us.

But, like physical training, we must be diligent in their application. God has not promised to shield us from trouble, but He has promised to protect us in the midst of trouble. Most of all, never forget that because of Christ's death and resurrection, Satan is already a defeated foe—and someday the war will be over.

July 14

BEYOND THE STARRY SKY

We are looking for the city that is to come.

HEBREWS 13:14, NRSV

Paul looked forward to death with great anticipation. He said, "For to me, to live is Christ, and to die is gain" (Phil. 1:21). Death for him was not an enemy to be feared, but a reality to be welcomed, in God's time. For him death was the joyous gateway to new life—the life of Heaven.

Without the resurrection of Christ there could be no hope for the future. The Bible promises that someday we are going to stand face to face with the resurrected Christ. All our questions will be answered, and all our sorrows and fears will vanish. An old gospel hymn puts it well:

Face to face with Christ my Savior,
Face to face, what will it be?
When with rapture I behold Him,
Jesus Christ who died for me?
Face to face I shall behold Him,
Far beyond the starry sky;
Face to face in all His glory
I shall see Him by and by.

—Carrie E. Breck

July 15

THE BLESSING OF BURDENS

The Lord has comforted His people and will
have compassion on His suffering ones.
ISAIAH 49:13, NRSV

Comfort and prosperity have never enriched
the world as much as adversity. Out of pain
and problems have come the sweetest songs,
the most poignant poems, the most gripping stories,
and inspiring lives.

Yet it is hard to think about this when troubles
overwhelm us or uncertainty and fear grip our hearts.
Our problems are real, and it is difficult in the heat of
the moment to think of anything else.

Our oldest daughter married a Swiss, and they
often spend their summers in Switzerland. Sometimes
we have visited them there and have gone soaring
above the countryside on chair lifts high in the
Alps. Looking down we can see almost a carpet of
wildflowers, some of the most beautiful in the world.
Only a few months before, those plants were buried
under heavy snow. Yet that snow prepared the way
for their growth—providing them with water, and
even insulating them from the winter winds. Our
burdens can be like that snow, preparing the way for
something beautiful once the winter is past.

Only One Way

Whoever desires, let him take the water of life freely.
REVELATION 22:17

A driver stopped to ask the way to a certain street. When told, he asked doubtfully, "Is that the best way?" The man replied, "That is the *only* way."

There is only one way of salvation—and that is Christ. Jesus said, "No one comes to the Father except through Me" (John 14:6). Peter declared, "There is no other name under heaven given among men by which we must be saved" (Acts 4:12).

Is this arrogance or intolerance? No—and Christians must never be guilty of those attitudes. We are saved solely by God's grace; we do not deserve it. But Christ was God's appointed means of salvation. Only Christ died for our sins; only Christ rose from the dead.

God's offer of forgiveness and new life still stands. If you have never done so, turn to Christ today. And if you do know Him, pray today for someone you know who does not yet believe, and ask God to help you tell that person of His salvation.

July 17

COMMITTED LOVE

Perfect love casts out fear.
1 JOHN 4:18

When I understand something of Christ's love for me as a sinner, I respond with love for Christ—and that love includes feelings and emotions.

But emotions come and go, and we must not allow them to mislead us. God loves me, whether I "feel" it or not. Christians who gauge their relationship with Christ only by their feelings seldom have a stable spiritual life.

What makes the difference? It can be summarized in one word: commitment. Feelings come and go, but commitment stays. (The same should be true in a marriage.) We who have committed our lives to Christ may feel joy, gratitude, love, and so on. But even when we don't have those feelings, our commitment keeps us true to Christ.

This commitment not only keeps us faithful to Christ when we don't feel like it; it also keeps away negative emotions such as doubt and fear. John Witherspoon, the only cleric to sign the Declaration of Independence, once said, "It is only the fear of God that can deliver us from the fear of man."

A Higher Destiny

The way of the Lord is strength for the upright.
Proverbs 10:29

Because God is the giver and source of life, He has a legitimate claim upon our lives. He is our Heavenly Father, and He has the right to expect us to be His loyal and loving children. Because I am His child, He also longs to have fellowship with me.

The story of the Prodigal Son (which you can read in Luke 15:11 ff.) is a revelation of God's desire for human fellowship. He yearns over His children who have wandered far from Him and longs for them to come home and be near to Him.

All through the Bible we see God's patience and perseverance as He pursues misguided and obstinate men and women—men and women who were born to a high destiny as His sons and daughters, but who strayed from His side. From Genesis to Revelation God is constantly saying, "Return to Me, and I will return to you."

No matter how far you have strayed, God still loves you, and He wants to welcome you home—forever.

July 19

THE BIBLE IS TRUE

Forever, O Lord, Your word is settled in heaven.
PSALM 119:89

As we survey the world scene with Bible in hand, we know we do not worship an absentee God. He is standing in the shadows of history, still working to bring His plans to completion.

Therefore we are not disturbed by the pictures of chaos, violence, bloodshed, and war that fill our television screens and flood our newspapers. We know these are the consequences of humanity's evil and sin, caused by our rebellion against God. Every headline, every news report confirms what the prophet Jeremiah said centuries ago: "The heart is deceitful above all things, and desperately wicked; who can know it?" (Jer. 17:9).

But never forget: *God* will speak history's final word. Every day the world moves closer to the time when Christ will return, Satan will be defeated, and God's perfect plan will be fulfilled.

No matter how foreboding the future, the Christian knows the end of the story—and it is glorious! Don't lose heart. The best is yet to be!

July 20

VALUABLE TO GOD

He who trusts in his riches will fall,
but the righteous will flourish like foliage.
PROVERBS 11:28

A certain rich man died and the question was asked at his funeral, "How much did he leave?" "He left it all," came the reply.

Often, I hear someone introduced this way: "This is Bob and he works for . . . ," as if where a person works or what a person does determines his or her value. (I have noticed it is usually only the well-to-do or those who are thought of as "successful" who are introduced this way.)

Yet God does not judge us by our success. He loves each person the same. Your value and mine does not come from what we do, the clothes we wear, the house we live in, or the type of car we drive. Our value comes from the fact that God made us and loves us, and Christ died for us. Our value comes from the fact that He adopted us into His family, and we are now His children forever.

Don't depend on possessions or position for your identity. Get your identity from Christ, for you are of infinite worth to Him!

July 21

VICTORY IN JESUS

Thanks be to God, who gives us the
victory through our Lord Jesus Christ.
1 CORINTHIANS 15:57, NRSV

Haydn, the great musician, was once asked why his church music was so cheerful. He replied, "When I think upon God, my heart is so full of joy that the notes dance and leap, as it were, from my pen, and since God has given me a cheerful heart, it will be pardoned me that I serve Him with a cheerful spirit."

Haydn had discovered the secret to lasting joy: "I think on God." Looking at our circumstances won't bring us lasting joy. It may even make us depressed or angry. But when we "think on God"—when we turn our minds and hearts to His power and His love for us, we can't help but be joyful. Paul said, "Set your mind on things above, not on things on the earth" (Col. 3:2). Discouragement flees in the face of joy.

Every day brings battles and temptations. But the strength we need for conquering them comes from Christ. We can do like the little girl who said that when the devil came knocking with a temptation, she just sent Jesus to the door!

July 22

LOOK TO GOD

Lift up your heads, because your redemption draws near.
LUKE 21:28

I f you've ever flown in an airplane you know that your perspective of the earth is far different from what it was when you were on the ground. Pictures of the earth that have been taken from the moon and from space show an earth that looks much different from what we see down here.

This is the kind of perspective God wants to give us concerning our lives. As we look to God, instead of to ourselves and our circumstances, our perspectives change.

Don't get bogged down in the circumstances of life. At the moment we see only our immediate problems and burdens, but God sees the whole. He sees not only the present, but the future as well. He wants to lift us above ourselves. He wants us to see everything in light of His plans. The Psalmist said, "The LORD will perfect that which concerns me" (Ps. 138:8).

Don't get bogged down. Keep your eyes on God, for He sees the whole picture, and He knows what is best for you. You can trust Him, because He loves you.

July 23

A Solid Foundation

The Lord is my rock and my fortress and my deliverer.
2 SAMUEL 22:2

My children used to sing a song in Sunday school classes: "The wise man built his house upon the rock . . ." The wise man does build his house upon the rock—the Lord Jesus Christ and His Word—for nothing built of or on any other substance will stand the test of time.

In big cities I often see wrecking balls destroying old structures to make way for new ones. Some of these "old structures" in America are less than a hundred years old. In Europe, buildings several centuries old are common. But even these buildings will eventually be destroyed, by a natural disaster if not by man.

Only what is built on the solid foundation of Christ will last. Jesus said, "Everyone who hears these words of mine and puts them into practice is like a wise man who built his house on the rock" (Matt. 7:24, NIV). Are you listening to God's Word and putting it into practice every day?

A Gentle Kindness

*The Lord's servant must not be
quarrelsome but kindly to every one.*

2 TIMOTHY 2:24, NRSV

Jesus was a gentle and compassionate person.
When He came into the world, there were few
hospitals, few places of refuge for the poor,
few homes for orphans. There were no hospitals to
treat the mentally ill, no shelters for the homeless. In
comparison to today, it was a cruel world.

Christ changed all that. He healed the sick, fed
the hungry, and opened the eyes of the blind. He
commanded His disciples, "Love your neighbor
as yourself" (Matt. 19:19), and taught them to
observe what we have come to call the Golden
Rule: "In everything, do to others what you would
have them do to you" (Matt. 7:12, NIV). Wherever
true Christianity has gone, His followers have
performed acts of kindness, love, and gentleness.

Do others see Christ's gentleness and compassion
in you?

July 25

OVERCOMING TRIBULATION

You will have tribulation; but be of good cheer,
I have overcome the world.
JOHN 16:33

When trials come, we sometimes act as if God is on vacation. We question God: Why is this happening to me? What did I do to deserve this? Why am I going through this difficult circumstance? What's wrong with You, God?!

But such complaining is shortsighted and wrong. God is far higher than we are. Who are we to say He is wrong, or to tell Him what He ought to be doing? As God reminded Job, "Where were you when I laid the foundations of the earth?" (Job 38:4). Such complaining also shows a lack of faith; we are doubting God's wisdom and His love for us.

Read the promises of Scripture for the answer. Jesus said, "In the world you will have tribulation." He didn't say that you could have tribulation or that if you aren't a good person, tribulation will come your way. Jesus flatly stated you *will* have tribulation. It is as certain as growing older.

But the wonderful promise of Christ is that while you will have trials and tribulations, "Be of good cheer. I have overcome the world."

JOY ON THE JOURNEY

The joy of the Lord is your strength.
NEHEMIAH 8:10

Some people have a warped idea of living the Christian life. Seeing talented, successful Christians, they attempt to imitate them. For them, the grass on the other side of the fence is always greener. But when they discover that their own gifts are different or their contributions are more modest (or even invisible), they collapse in discouragement and overlook genuine opportunities that are open to them. They have forgotten that they are here to serve Christ, not themselves.

Be like the apostle Paul and say, "None of these things move me." Few men suffered as Paul did, yet he learned how to live above his circumstances—even in a prison cell. You can do the same. The key is to realize you are here to serve Christ, not yourself.

God does not promise us an easy life, free of troubles, trials, difficulties, and temptations. He never promises that life will be perfect. He does not call His children to a playground, but to a battleground. In the midst of it all, when we serve Christ, we truly discover that "the joy of the LORD is [our] strength."

July 27

A Victorious Christian

The Spirit also helps in our weaknesses.
ROMANS 8:26

We need to rely constantly on the Holy Spirit. We need to remember that Christ dwells in us through the Holy Spirit. Our bodies are the dwelling place of the Third Person of the Trinity.

Why don't we rely on Him as we should? We don't realize how weak we are. We don't realize how strong our enemy is. We may even doubt if God is really going to help us. Or we think we can do it all ourselves—or that we must.

But we should ask Him to do it all and to take over in our lives. We should tell Him how weak, helpless, unstable, and unreliable we are. It is important that we stand aside and let Him take over in all our choices and decisions. We know that the Holy Spirit prays for us (Rom. 8:26), and what a comfort that should be to the weakest of us.

A victorious Christian is one who, in spite of worries, inner conflicts, and tensions, is confident that God is in control and will be victorious in the end. Whatever our difficulties, whatever our circumstances, we must remember, as Corrie ten Boom used to say, "Jesus is victor!"

FREE TO CHOOSE

Choose this day whom you will serve.
JOSHUA 24:15, NRSV

Repeatedly in the Bible, both nations and individuals had to make decisions affecting their futures—and so do we. Sometimes they made wrong choices and suffered the consequences as a result.

When we face decisions, we need to remember that God hasn't left us in the dark, nor is He uninterested. God loves us, and He wants what is best for us. He has a perfect path in life for us, and He wants us to choose it instead of the wrong paths Satan would tempt us to follow.

Even when our way seems unclear, God gives us light. He gives us His Word, the Bible—and many of our decisions would be much easier if we only knew its moral and spiritual principles. He also gives us wisdom (sometimes through other people) to understand our situation, and He gives us the Holy Spirit to guide us.

Never make a decision without committing it to God and seeking His will. He promises to guide you—and He will.

July 29

Simple Trust

Trust in the Lord with all your heart,
and lean not on your own understanding.
Proverbs 3:5

There will always be secrets and motives of God that lie beyond our grasp. God knows everything; we do not. Only in Heaven will we understand God's ways more fully. As Paul said, "Now I know in part, but then I shall know just as I also am known" (1 Cor. 13:12).

But based upon what we do know about God's character, demonstrated supremely in the Cross, we can trust that God is doing what is best for us. God says in His Word, "I know the plans I have for you... plans to prosper you and not to harm you, plans to give you hope and a future" (Jer. 29:11, NIV).

As Corrie ten Boom once explained, "Picture a piece of embroidery placed between you and God, with the right side up toward God. Man sees the loose, frayed ends; but God sees the pattern."

God is in control. Whatever comes into our lives, we can confidently say, "We know that all things work together for good to those who love God, to those who are the called according to His purpose" (Rom. 8:28).

THE LIGHT OF LIFE

Your faith and hope are in God.
1 PETER 1:21, NIV

We get so used to this world that we lose sight of the next. We get so used to the darkness and chaos of this world's suffering and violence that we lose sight of the brightness of Him who alone could say, "I am the light of the world. He who follows Me shall not walk in darkness, but have the light of life" (John 8:12).

He alone is "the Lamb of God, who takes away the sin of the world!" (John 1:29). He alone is the Hope of the hopeless, the Savior of the lost, the Guide of the wandering. He alone is "the radiance of God's glory and the exact representation of his being, sustaining all things by his powerful word" (Heb. 1:3, NIV).

Today world leaders struggle with almost insurmountable problems—and they always will. But in the midst of this world's persistent darkness, never lose sight of Jesus. He alone is the hope of the world—and He is your hope as well.

July 31

EFFECTIVE PRAYER

Before they call, I will answer; and while
they are still speaking, I will hear.
ISAIAH 65:24

John Knox spent much time in prayer, and the
Church in Scotland burst into new life. John
Wesley prayed long and often, and the Methodist movement was born. Martin Luther prayed earnestly, and the Reformation exploded across Europe.

Why was prayer so important to these spiritual giants of the past? Because they knew they were up against almost overwhelming forces of spiritual opposition. They also knew the urgency of the Gospel message, and that prayer was an essential weapon in advancing the Gospel to the ends of the earth. Like Paul, they knew that "the weapons of our warfare are not carnal but mighty in God for pulling down strongholds" (2 Cor. 10:4). Is our situation any different today?

God desires that we Christians be concerned and burdened for a lost world. If we pray this kind of prayer, an era of peace may come to the world and wickedness may be turned back. "The effective, fervent prayer of a righteous man avails much" (James 5:16).

August

*Pray for a sense of urgency to grip
the hearts of Christ's followers
for their lost family members,
friends, and neighbors.*

August 1

PRAYER RELEASES GOD'S POWER

Pray without ceasing.
1 THESSALONIANS 5:17

How many times have you heard someone say, "All I can do is pray"?

All I can do is pray?! You might as well say to a starving man, "All I can do is offer you food," or to a sick person, "All I can do is give you medicine that will make you well," or to a poor child, "All I can do is buy the toy you most want for your birthday."

Praying unlocks the doors of Heaven and releases the power of God. James 4:2 says, "You do not have because you do not ask." The Bible says, "Be anxious for nothing, but in everything by prayer and supplication, with thanksgiving, let your requests be made known to God" (Phil. 4:6).

This is true not only for our needs but the needs of others. So often our prayers focus only on ourselves. But God wants to use us, through our prayers, to touch the lives of other people as well. For whom should you be praying this day?

Choose Life

I have set before you life and death,
... therefore choose life.

Deuteronomy 30:19

Before the space shuttle program, American ships and helicopters used to recover astronauts whose space capsules had parachuted into the sea. The tiny spacecraft would be located in the enormous ocean, and the astronauts would be lifted out of their capsule into the helicopter, which would then fly them to the safety of the ship.

I often thought, as I watched those scenes on television, how like God this operation was. God hovers over the entire world, seeking to pluck from sin immortal souls who are in danger of "drowning" in hell. He tosses out a line to all those who are in trouble. Some grab on to God's line and freely receive the gift of His Son, Jesus Christ. They are pulled to safety, and, eventually, taken to Heaven.

But others ignore the line, or even knock it away, believing they are not really in peril, or that they can make it to safety on their own. Tragically, they are lost not because God has rejected them, but because they have rejected God.

Don't make the wrong choice!

August 3

CHRIST—OUR EXAMPLE

He learned obedience by the things which He suffered.
HEBREWS 5:8

The main reason Jesus died on the cross was to save us from our sins. But the New Testament also stresses the importance of His suffering as an example for us.

The Greek word for *example* comes from ancient school life, and refers to something written down by the teacher, so it could be followed and copied exactly by a child learning to write. Christ is our copybook. We look to Him as our teacher, and by His suffering He gave us an example to follow, so we can learn how suffering is to be borne.

How did He bear it? By not giving in to despair or doubt. By looking beyond it and seeing the glory that was to come. By knowing the Father was with Him and would use His suffering for good. The same can be true for us.

The author of Hebrews writes, "Consider him who endured such opposition from sinners, so that you will not grow weary and lose heart" (Heb. 12:3, NIV). Yes, *consider Him.*

August 4

PATIENCE AND PERFECTION

The testing of your faith produces patience.
JAMES 1:3

Patience isn't easy for most of us. If a plane is delayed a few minutes or something doesn't happen exactly when or how we expected it to, we get impatient and frustrated. I have heard of people who quit going to a particular church because the preacher didn't stop exactly on time! James said, "Be *patient*, then, brothers and sisters, until the Lord's coming. See how the farmer waits for the land to yield its valuable crop, *patiently* waiting for the autumn and spring rains. You too, be *patient* and stand firm, because the Lord's coming is near" (James 5:7–8, italics mine, NIV).

Patience is not simply "teeth-clenched" endurance. It is an attitude of expectation. The farmer patiently watches his barren ground because he knows there will be results. He has patience in his labors because there will be products of his labor.

So it is in the spiritual realm. God knows the final product of what is happening to us, and He would have us link patience to our faith. Ask God for the gift of patience—and then use it.

August 5

PEACE ON EARTH?

He Himself is our peace.

EPHESIANS 2:14

For as long as I can remember there have been innovative ideas for bringing peace to this earth. Organizations have been created, much money and time have been spent, treaties have been signed, books have been written—all in an effort to find a formula that would bring peace on earth and good will to men.

World War I was called "the war to end all wars," but it wasn't. Whether men shoot and fight one another or not, there is "warfare" in the home: warfare between husband and wife, between parents and children, between brothers and sisters, between neighbors, between boss and employee.

What can be done? It sounds almost simplistic to say we need to turn to God—but that is the only lasting solution. Only God can remove the poisons of greed and hatred and jealousy in our hearts, and replace them with contentment and compassion and forgiveness. Only He can subdue the violence and anger that rage within us, and replace them with His peace and love.

Whatever wars rage in your life, lay them at the foot of the Cross and ask Jesus to give you His peace.

August 6

A HAPPY HOME

Children are a gift from God; they are his reward.
PSALM 127:3, TLB

Today there are more pressures on the home than perhaps at any other time in the history of the human race.

By necessity or by desire, more women are working today than ever before. Many feel guilty about leaving their children in the care of others or having them return to an empty home while they are at work. But many women (and men, too) still devote more attention to their working life than they do to their family life. Is it any wonder, then, that so many homes are in trouble?

What achievement in life is equal to a happy home and rearing successful children who grow up in praise of their parents? Every material goal, even if it is met, will pass away. But the heritage of children is timeless.

Our primary responsibility is to be sure our children grow up in homes where God is honored and the love of Christ reigns. Do your children sense that Christ is at the center of your home?

August 7

PRAY ABOUT YOUR PROBLEMS

Don't worry about anything;
instead, pray about everything.
PHILIPPIANS 4:6, TLB

What do you do when you have a problem? Do you worry? Most of us do. But does worrying solve the problem? No, it does not. Then if worry doesn't solve the problem, why worry?

The Bible's account about Hezekiah gives us an idea for problem solving: "Hezekiah received the letter from the hand of the messengers, and read it; and Hezekiah went up to the house of the LORD, and spread it before the LORD. Then Hezekiah prayed before the LORD" (2 Kings 19:14–15).

Instead of turning to God as a first resource, we so often turn to Him as a last resort. Follow Hezekiah's formula. Turn to God first with your problems, for only He is capable of handling them in a way that will be in your best interest—and according to His perfect will.

THE PROBLEM OF SUFFERING

I have kept His way and not turned aside.
JOB 23:11

Some scholars think Job may be the oldest book in the Bible. Whether that is true or not, it certainly deals with one of humanity's oldest questions: Why does God allow suffering?

It isn't an easy issue, because it goes to the heart of our deepest questions about God. After all (the argument runs), how could a loving and gracious God allow suffering? To put it another way, if God lets us suffer, He must not love us. But that conclusion is false. God does love us—and the proof is the suffering He allowed His Son to endure on the Cross.

What, then, is the answer to this age-old question? The key is to understand the character of God. That is what Job discovered. No, God never gave him a logical, complete answer for his suffering. But through his experience he came to realize that God could be trusted, because He is merciful and loving. And you can trust Him too—not because He always gives us all the answers, but simply because He is God.

August 9

JESUS' PRAYER PROGRAM

Whatever you ask the Father in
My name He will give you.
JOHN 16:23

O ne of the most amazing things in all the
Scriptures is how much time Jesus spent
in prayer. He had only three years of public
ministry, yet He was never too hurried to spend
hours in prayer. He prayed before every difficult task
confronting Him. He prayed with regularity—not a
day began or closed in which He did not unfold His
soul before His Father.

How quickly and carelessly, by contrast, we pray.
Snatches of memorized verses are hastily spoken in
the morning; then we say good-bye to God for the
rest of the day, until we rush through a few closing
petitions at night.

This is not the prayer program that Jesus outlined.
Jesus pleaded long and repeatedly. It is recorded
that He spent entire nights in fervent appeal. No one
could have been busier—but He was never too busy
for prayer.

What keeps you from making prayer a priority in
your schedule?

TRUST AND TOIL

*As the body without the spirit is dead,
so faith without works is dead also.*

JAMES 2:26

The Scriptures teach that a Christian is one who trusts Christ as Savior and obeys Him as Lord. That is the essence of Christian discipleship—believing and following. The book of Acts says, "The *disciples* were first called Christians in Antioch" (Acts 11:26).

The New Testament makes no separation between belief and obedience. They are linked together as one, because if you truly believe, you will truly follow. Trust makes us part of the Kingdom, but our love for God and obedience to His will are the badges of our citizenship in that Kingdom.

That is why the Christian life is a happy blend of trust and toil, resting and striving, receiving and doing. God does His part, and we must do ours. A farmer's crop is a gift from God—but it also requires hard work. God may give a person the gift of music—but it takes practice and discipline to make it come alive.

Is any area of your life "off limits" to Christ? Believe—and obey.

August 11

GOD, OUR FATHER

*I will be a Father to you, and you
shall be My sons and daughters.*
2 CORINTHIANS 6:18

In the familiar story of the Prodigal Son, the young
man was not satisfied to be in his father's house
with all of his needs met. He wanted more. He
believed the lie that something more exciting was in
store for him away from his father.

Isn't this how we sometimes behave—even as
Christians? We think that God is holding out on us,
that there is something better than a close relationship
with our Heavenly Father, that the world has more
excitement and fulfillment to offer us than God does.

But it isn't true. By thinking this way and then acting
on it—whether we go as far away as the Prodigal or
not—we create our own desperate circumstances.
Then we turn back to God, crying out for deliverance
and forgiveness.

Fortunately, our Heavenly Father always hears
our cries. Full repentance is always answered by full
forgiveness. But wouldn't it have been far better to
have avoided it in the first place? Don't ever—*ever*—
think Satan's way is better than God's way. It *never* is.

The Hope of Heaven

Precious in the sight of the Lord is the death of His saints.
PSALM 116:15

Death is the one experience through which we all will pass. We may meet it with resignation, denial, or even without a moment's thought—but come it will.

But death for the believer is distinctly different from what it is for the unbeliever. For us, it isn't something to be feared or shunned, for we know death is but the shadowed threshold to the palace of God. No wonder Paul declared, "I desire to depart and be with Christ, which is better by far" (Phil. 1:23, NIV).

Sometimes God gives His departing saints glimpses of Heaven (partly, I believe, to encourage those of us who remain). Just before dying my grandmother sat up in bed, smiled, and said, "I see Jesus, and He has His hand outstretched to me. And there is Ben, and he has both of his eyes and both of his legs." (Ben, my grandfather, had lost an eye and a leg at Gettysburg.)

Are you looking forward to that day when you will go to be with Christ, "which is better by far"?

August 13

EVERLASTING LOVE

I have loved you with an everlasting love; therefore with lovingkindness I have drawn you.
JEREMIAH 31:3

Who can describe or measure the love of God? Our Bible is a revelation of the fact that God is love. When we preach justice, it is justice tempered with love. When we preach righteousness, it is righteousness founded on love. When we preach atonement for sin, it is atonement necessitated because of love, provided by love, finished by love.

When we preach the resurrection of Christ, we are preaching the miracle of love. When we preach the abiding presence of Christ, we are preaching the power of love. When we preach the return of Christ, we are preaching the fulfillment of love.

No matter what sin we have committed, no matter how black, dirty, shameful, or terrible it may be, God loves us. We may be at the very gate of hell itself, but God loves us with an everlasting love. The proof? Jesus Christ, God's only Son, went to the Cross for us. "For God so loved the world that He gave His only begotten Son, that whoever believes in Him should not perish but have eternal life" (John 3:16).

August 14

THE WORK OF ANGELS

Bless the Lord, you His angels,
who excel in strength, who do His word.
PSALM 103:20

I t's natural to concentrate on what the angels do for us, these who are "sent to serve those who will inherit salvation" (Heb. 1:14, NIV).

But the Bible indicates the angels do much more than that. Especially, we are told, the angels unite in constant praise to God, giving glory to His name and rejoicing in His holiness and perfection. "Bless the LORD, you His angels."

Isaiah is granted a vision of Heaven, where the angelic hosts proclaim, "Holy, holy, holy is the LORD of hosts; the whole earth is full of His glory!" (Isa. 6:3). John sees "many angels around the throne . . . saying with a loud voice: 'Worthy is the Lamb who was slain'" (Rev. 5:11–12). Jesus said there is "rejoicing in the presence of the angels of God over one sinner who repents" (Luke 15:10, NIV).

Are they not examples to us? Shouldn't rejoicing and praise be hallmarks of our lives? Praise will banish darkness, and bring us closer to God. Martin Luther once said, "Come, let us sing a psalm and drive away the devil!"

August 15

FULL SURRENDER

Whoever loses his life for My sake . . . will save it.
MARK 8:35

A police sergeant once asked me the secret of victorious Christian living. I told him there is no magic formula. But if any one word could describe it, it would be *surrender*.

You may ask, "How can I surrender my life?" It is surrendered in the same way that salvation comes to the sinner. There needs to be confession of sin and a complete yielding of every area of our lives, personalities, and wills to Jesus Christ—plus faith that Christ will accept that commitment.

It's not enough for us to be confirmed or to make a decision for Christ at an altar. We cannot walk successfully in the glow of that experience for the rest of our lives. We need to return and renew those vows and covenants with the Lord. We need to take inventory and have regular spiritual checkups.

Jesus said, "If anyone desires to come after Me, let him deny himself, and take up his cross daily, and follow Me" (Luke 9:23). *Daily* surrender—that's the key to daily victory.

August 16

Fervent Prayer

If my people . . . will . . . pray and seek
my face, . . . I will hear from heaven.
2 Chronicles 7:14

From one end of the Bible to the other, there is the record of those whose prayers were answered—men and women who turned the tide of history by prayer, who fervently prayed, and God answered.

Elijah prayed, and God sent fire from Heaven to consume the offering on the altar he had built in the presence of God's enemies. Elisha prayed, and the son of the Shunammite woman was raised from the dead. Hannah prayed and God gave her a son, Samuel, who would bless God's people for decades.

Paul prayed, and dozens of churches were born in Asia Minor and Europe. Peter prayed, and Dorcas was raised to life, to have added years of service for Jesus Christ.

Their prayers were the natural outflow of their deep inner faith. Their prayers were part of a greater whole: godly lives lived for God's glory. As the seventeenth century theologian, John Owen, said, "He who prays as he ought, will endeavor to live as he prays."

August 17

LORD AND MASTER

You call Me Teacher and Lord,
and you say well, for so I am.
JOHN 13:13

I wonder if you've ever thought about the incredible number of messages that rain down on us every day: television ads, e-mails, phone calls, magazines, junk mail, videos, billboards, conversations—the list is almost endless.

How many of those shape our thinking? How many of them subtly convince us that the road to happiness is really paved with possessions, or beauty, or money, or fame, or any of a hundred other things? How many of them persuade us that the most important thing in life is financial success, or the esteem of others, or power, or sex? It's hard to resist the cumulative impact of so many messages.

But God says our thinking must be shaped by His truth. What this world calls valuable, God calls worthless. What this world scorns, God exalts. "My thoughts are not your thoughts, nor are your ways My ways" (Isa. 55:8).

Jesus said, "You call Me Teacher and Lord, and you say well, for so I am." Is He *your* Teacher and Lord—or is the world?

August 18

HOPE FOR THE HEART

My heart is glad, and . . .
my flesh also will rest in hope.
PSALM 16:9

Perhaps the greatest psychological, spiritual, and medical need that all people have is the need for hope. Dr. McNair Wilson, the famous cardiologist, remarked in his autobiography, *Doctor's Progress*, "Hope is the medicine I use more than any other—hope can cure nearly anything."

Years ago Dr. Harold Wolff, professor of medicine at Cornell University Medical College and associate professor of psychiatry, said, "Hope, like faith and a purpose in life, is medicinal. This is not a statement of belief, but a conclusion proved by meticulously controlled scientific experiment."

When hope dies, despair will overwhelm us. Hope is both biologically and psychologically vital to us. Men and women must have hope—and true hope comes only from Christ. He gives us hope for the future as we turn in faith to Him—hope for eternity, and hope right now.

August 19

LOVING COMPASSION

In this is love, not that we loved God,
but that He loved us.
1 JOHN 4:10

"The supreme happiness of life," Victor Hugo said, "is the conviction that we are loved." "Love is the first requirement for mental health," declared Sigmund Freud.

Unfortunately, many people go through life feeling unloved—and unlovable. Perhaps they were constantly criticized or ignored as children, or their family was torn by conflict. Perhaps they made bad choices about important issues in life—which only confirmed their belief that they were unworthy of love. This may be your experience.

But listen: I have good news! No matter the reason, your feelings aren't telling you the truth! God loves you, and if you begin to see yourself the way God sees you, your attitudes will begin to change. If He didn't love you, would Christ have been willing to die for you? But He did! The Bible says, "By this we know love, because He laid down His life for us" (1 John 3:16).

God loves you. Hammer that truth into your heart and mind every day. It will make all the difference.

FACING REJECTION

He is despised and rejected by men, a Man
of sorrows and acquainted with grief.
ISAIAH 53:3

Throughout His earthly life, Jesus was constantly exposed to personal criticism and rejection. At the beginning of His ministry, His own townsfolk at Nazareth tried to hurl Him down from the brow of the hill (Luke 4:29). The religious and political leaders constantly argued with Him and conspired to kill Him. At length He was arrested and brought to trial before Pilate and Herod. Even though He was guiltless of the accusations, He was denounced as an enemy of God and man, and not worthy to live.

How did He respond to criticism and rejection? First, with *steadfastness*. He did not tone down His message, nor did He stop doing what He knew was right. Second, with *strength*. Ahead of Him was the Cross—but He did not lose courage or shrink from what He knew was God's will. Third, with *submission*. When Herod prodded Him to defend Himself, "He answered him nothing" (Luke 23:9). Only one thing mattered: Fulfilling God's purpose for His life.

How will we meet criticism?

August 21

THE WAY OF MEEKNESS

Blessed are the meek for they shall inherit the earth.
MATTHEW 5:5

No person is meek by nature. We insist on our own way (even if we are mild-mannered by nature), and if anyone blocks our path we react with hurt, anger, resentment, and even revenge.

Moses was meek, but he was not meek by nature. God worked meekness into his life over a forty-year period.

Peter was certainly not meek by nature. He was impetuous, saying and doing the first thing that came into his mind. But little by little, the Holy Spirit of God transformed Peter after the resurrection of Jesus.

Before his conversion, Paul was not meek. His job was to persecute Christians! Yet Paul wrote to the church at Galatia, "The fruit of the Spirit is . . . gentleness, goodness . . . meekness" (Gal. 5:22–23, KJV).

It is our human nature to be proud and self-assertive, not meek. Only the Spirit of God can transform our lives through the new birth experience and then make us over again into the image of Christ. He is our example of true meekness.

THE REALITY OF HEAVEN

God will wipe away every tear from their eyes.
REVELATION 7:17

In the midst of his suffering Job said, "Man is born to trouble as surely as sparks fly upward" (Job 5:7, NIV). It is true. I have never met a person who did not have troubles of some kind. Fear and sickness rob us of happiness; broken relationships and shattered dreams destroy our peace.

But one of God's greatest promises is that all of these will be forgotten in Heaven, where "there shall be no more death, nor sorrow, nor crying. There shall be no more pain, for the former things have passed away" (Rev. 21:4).

This is the supreme reality of Heaven. Throughout eternity there will be an intimate relationship between Christ and His church. He will be the Lamb who is in the midst of the throne, and He shall lead them to fountains of living waters.

With this great certainty and assurance, the future holds no terrors we cannot face. Beyond the crisis lies Heaven and the utopia of our dreams. Thus the Christian should never be filled with fear, discouragement, or despondency. Ahead of us is Heaven!

August 23

TRULY TRANSFORMED

Present your bodies a living sacrifice....
And be not conformed to this world.
ROMANS 12:1-2

Others can't see what goes on inside of you—your thoughts and emotions, your dreams and motives. Nor can they "see" your inner commitment to Christ.

All they can see is your body—and they will judge what is on the inside of you by what they see happening on the outside. A frown signals concern or disapproval; a smile signals gratitude or welcome; a clenched fist signals hostility or anger.

Do you see why Paul tells us to "present [our] bodies a living sacrifice"? The reason is simple: The way we use our bodies will signal to others what we really are on the inside. We may claim to follow Christ, but if our actions tell a different story, people have a right to question our claim. Our dress, our speech, our habits—all should honor Christ. We are to be "blameless and pure, 'children of God without fault in a warped and crooked generation'" (Phil. 2:15, NIV).

Do your outer actions signal your inner commitment to Christ?

August 24

PURE IN HEART

Blessed are the pure in heart, for they shall see God.
MATTHEW 5:8

Why does Jesus say we should be "pure *in heart*"? The reason is because our heart—our inner being—is the root of all our actions. From our hearts come our motives, our desires, our goals, our emotions. If our hearts aren't right, neither will be our actions.

Jesus put it this way: "From within, out of the heart of men, proceed evil thoughts, adulteries, fornications, murders, thefts, covetousness, wickedness, deceit, lewdness, an evil eye, blasphemy, pride, foolishness" (Mark 7:21–22). Not a very pretty picture!

But God wants to give us a pure heart—and He will. He does this first of all when we turn to Christ in repentance and faith, for "the blood of Jesus Christ His Son cleanses us from all sin" (1 John 1:7). But He does it also day by day, as we submit to the Holy Spirit and—with His help—flee from evil and seek what is good. "Blessed are the pure *in heart*."

August 25

HE STILL SUSTAINS US

The eternal God is your refuge.
DEUTERONOMY 33:27

When we hear the word *suffering* we usually think of physical pain. But psychological suffering is just as real—and sometimes more devastating.

It may be an inner grief or sorrow you cannot express, even to your dearest friend or spouse. It may sap your strength or paralyze you with anxiety. It may harm your relationships, or even grip you so tightly that it becomes more than just a temporary problem, but a serious psychological illness.

Paul knew what it was to experience psychological suffering; he told the Corinthians he had written them "out of much affliction and anguish of heart" (2 Cor. 2:4). Jesus in the Garden of Gethsemane, "being in agony, . . . prayed more earnestly" (Luke 22:44). After denying His Lord three times, Peter "went out and wept bitterly" (Luke 22:62).

But when such times come (and they come to us all) God still loves us. He does not abandon us. Remember: "The eternal God is your refuge, and underneath are the everlasting arms" (Deut. 33:27).

August 26

GOD IS OUR STRENGTH

The Lord is my light and my salvation;
whom shall I fear?

PSALM 27:1

I t is a *fact* that the Lord is my light and my salvation. So why should I be afraid? Since the Lord fears nothing, why should we fear?

The Scripture also declares that God is a "very present help in trouble" (Ps. 46:1). If we can't trust the all-powerful, all-knowing, all-loving God of the universe to help us, where can we turn? But we *can* trust Him!

God is able, indeed He is anxious, to deliver us from all sorts of trouble. He wants to give us strength to overcome the temptation to sin that separates Him from those He loves. He wants to give us the courage to confront our problems (instead of avoiding them or denying them), and then to find the practical wisdom and help we need to deal with them.

What do you fear today? Failure? Rejection? An illness or physical danger? The uncertainty of the future? Whatever it is, ask God to help you turn it over to Him. "The LORD is my light and my salvation; whom shall I fear?"

August 27

THE DIVINE "FIRE"

I will give them a new heart and a new mind.
EZEKIEL 11:19, TEV

When a person comes in contact with the living God, he or she can never be the same again. This divine "fire" either draws or drives, saves or destroys, helps or hinders. Accepted and utilized, it becomes a boon and a blessing. Rejected, it becomes a bane and a curse.

One dying thief was drawn to the warmth of the Savior; he responded in faith and was saved. The other dying thief turned away and rejected God's compassion; he was lost forever.

God takes the weak and makes them strong. He takes the vile and makes them clean. He takes the worthless and makes them worthwhile. He takes the sinful and makes them pure.

With this in mind, Ezekiel said, "Thus saith the LORD God . . . I will give them a new heart and a new mind. I will take away their stubborn heart of stone and will give them an obedient heart" (Eze. 11:19, TEV).

No, you will never be the same once you know Christ. What difference will He make in your life today?

AN ATTITUDE OF GRATITUDE

*Let the peace of Christ rule
in your hearts. . . . And be thankful.*
COLOSSIANS 3:15, NIV

Thankfulness isn't our usual response when something goes wrong. We may have a hundred good things for which to be thankful—but let one bad thing happen, and it's all we think about!

But the Bible says, "in *everything* give thanks" (1 Thess. 5:18). No matter what happens, we are to give thanks. Cultivate a spirit of thanksgiving in your life. Thank God for every blessing He gives you. Thank Him for Christ and what He has done for you. Even when things go wrong, thank Him that they aren't worse and you are still in His hands.

Having an attitude of thankfulness in all of life's circumstances will help you react as old Matthew Henry did when he was mugged. He wrote in his diary, "Let me be thankful first because I was never robbed before; second, although they took my purse, they did not take my life; third, because although they took my all, it was not much; and fourth, because it was I who was robbed, not I who robbed."

I wonder if I could be that thankful!

August 29

PERFECT PEACE

The love of God has been poured out in our hearts by the Holy Spirit who was given to us.
ROMANS 5:5

Years ago when I traveled to Europe to preach I liked to travel by sea, to enjoy the five days of relative quiet on the ship.

On one of my voyages Captain Anderson of the *United States* took me down to see the ship's gyroscope. He said, "When the sea is rough, the gyroscope helps to keep the ship on an even keel. Though the waves may reach tremendous proportions, the gyroscope helps to stabilize the vessel and maintain a high degree of equilibrium."

As I listened, I thought how like the gyroscope is the Holy Spirit in our hearts. Let the storms of life break over our heads. Let the enemy Satan come in like a flood. Let the waves of sorrow, suffering, temptation, and testing be unleashed upon us. Our souls will be kept on an even keel and in perfect peace when the Holy Spirit dwells in our hearts. He comforts us with God's abiding presence, and assures us that God's promises are true.

DIAMONDS IN THE DARK

Blessed is the man who fears the Lord, who delights greatly in His commandments.
PSALM 112:1

We Christians should stand out like sparkling diamonds against a dark velvet background. We should be more wholesome than anyone else. We should be poised, cultured, courteous, gracious—but firm in the things we do or do not do. We should laugh and be radiant; but we should refuse to allow the unbelieving world to pull us down to its level.

Christ meant for His followers to be different—and if they are truly following Him, they will be. But merely being different is not enough. We are to be the cleanest, the most holy, the kindest, the most unselfish, the friendliest, the most courteous, the most industrious, the most thoughtful, the truest, and the most loving people on earth. The Bible says, "Those who are wise will shine like the brightness of the heavens, and those who lead many to righteousness, like the stars for ever and ever" (Dan. 12:3, NIV).

Dr. Albert Schweitzer, the great missionary doctor and statesman, once said, "To be glad instruments of God's love in this imperfect world is the service to which man is called."

August 31

SERVANTS WHO SERVE

There remains therefore a rest for the people of God.
HEBREWS 4:9

We are the most entertained generation in history. Television sets pull in hundreds of channels; professional sports teams and pop music groups take in (and spend) billions of dollars; millions of people own second and third homes for vacations; our children are upset if they don't get the latest computer games for Christmas.

I believe this frantic search for entertainment is a symptom of something deeper. Some have suggested we are the most bored generation in history—and perhaps they are right. Down inside is an empty place in our hearts—a restlessness, a search for inner peace and tranquility—that will not go away. The irony is, the more we try to satisfy it, the less content we become.

Only Christ can fill that empty space in our hearts, and He will as we open our lives to Him. But God's Word also points us to the future—to Heaven, where our restless hearts will be at peace. "There remains therefore a rest for the people of God."

September

Pray that people you invite to your home will come and that God will open their hearts.

September 1

A TIME APART

The eyes of the Lord are on the righteous,
and His ears are open to their prayers.
1 PETER 3:12

Many people want to work *for* God, but they don't want to spend time *with* God. They are content with busyness instead of calmness, walking quietly in the presence of a Friend.

God calls us to work for Him, of course; there is no place in the Christian life for laziness or a lack of diligence. But God also calls us to Himself. He calls us to "Come with me by yourselves to a quiet place" (Mark 6:31, NIV).

Jesus, we read, "having risen a long while before daylight . . . went out and departed to a solitary place; and there He prayed" (Mark 1:35). If the Son of God needed time alone with His Father, how much more do we?

It is not easy to shut out the world, set aside a few minutes by yourself, and spend time in God's Word and prayer. But it is essential if we are to grow in our relationship with God and be strengthened for the battles ahead. Don't delay. Begin now to spend time alone with God every day.

September 2

OUR STUBBORN WILLS

Repent therefore and be converted.
ACTS 3:19

B ecoming a Christian is a once-for-all event, in which we repent of our sins and cast ourselves on Christ alone for our salvation. When we are converted, God takes us "out of darkness into His marvelous light" (1 Pet. 2:9).

But *being* a Christian is a daily, ongoing experience. It is a lifelong process of daily repentance and faith, turning from sin and seeking to live for Christ, in the power of the Holy Spirit.

That is where our wills come in. Although we have been converted and God has come to live in us, our old nature is still "alive and kicking." Our stubborn wills still demand to put self first instead of Christ.

It isn't easy to bring our stubborn wills into submission to Christ, but when we do, it is as if a misplaced vertebra has snapped back into place. Instead of the stress and tension of a life out of harmony with God, we discover the serenity of His presence.

Who will control your will today? You—or Christ?

September 3

WE NEED MERCY

The Lord is good; His mercy is everlasting.
PSALM 100:4

Many Christians do not see God in all of His wholeness. We glibly quote John 3:16—but we forget the following verses: "He who does not believe has been judged already"
(verse 18, NASB).

Yes, God is loving and compassionate. But He is also absolutely holy and pure, and because of that He is the Judge who will someday bring His full wrath to bear on those who refuse to repent.

All too often we are more afraid of physical pain than of moral wrong. The Cross is the proof that holiness is a principle for which God would die. God cannot clear the guilty until atonement is made. But that is what happened at the Cross.

Do not take sin lightly. Do not tolerate sin in your life, glibly saying, "Oh well, God will forgive it anyway." Sin is an offense to Almighty God, and while He will have mercy on us when we repent, He also is the Judge, and "everything is uncovered and laid bare before the eyes of him to whom we must give account" (Heb. 4:13, NIV).

September 4

GOD CONTROLS THE CLOCK

There is laid up for me the crown of righteousness.
2 TIMOTHY 4:8

Many people are asking, "Where is history heading?" A careful student of the Bible will see that God controls the clock of destiny. Amidst the world's confusion, God's omnipotent hand moves, working out His unchanging plan and purpose.

Not that we always see His hand at work. As the old English hymn writer William Cowper put it, "God moves in a mysterious way, His wonders to perform." God is not absent. By His providence He sustains us, and behind the scenes He is working to bring about His divine purpose.

What is that purpose? Paul recorded it this way: "That . . . He might gather together in one all things in Christ, both which are in heaven and which are on earth" (Eph. 1:10). Someday Satan's rule will be ended, and Christ will reign as Lord over all creation. Someday all the sin and rebellion of this corrupted universe will be destroyed, and Christ's kingdom of righteousness and peace will rule forever.

Don't be discouraged by what you see in the headlines every day. God is at work, and someday Christ will rule.

September 5

HOME AT LAST

Behold, I make all things new.
REVELATION 21:5

Heaven is a place so beautiful that when John, the apostle, caught a glimpse of it, the only thing to which he could liken it was a young woman on the crowning day of her life: her wedding day. He said that the holy city was like "a bride beautifully dressed for her husband" (Rev. 21:2, NIV).

Artists have tried to paint pictures of Heaven—but even the most impressive image falls far short of the reality. John's pen (under the inspiration of the Holy Spirit) could only hint at the splendor we shall see someday: "It shone with the glory of God, and its brilliance was like that of a very precious jewel, like a jasper, clear as crystal" (Rev. 21:11, NIV).

Yet the Bible's emphasis is not on Heaven's beauty but on Heaven's joy. The Bible teaches that Heaven will be a home that is happy because there will be nothing in it to hinder happiness. "And there shall by no means enter it anything that defiles. . . . But the throne of God and of the Lamb shall be in it" (Rev. 21:27; 22:3).

September 6

COMPASSION AND LOVE

*Beloved, if God so loved us, we also
ought to love one another.*

1 JOHN 4:11

Charles Allen once made this statement: "Some people seem to have such a passion for righteousness that they have no room left for compassion for those who have failed."

I pray that would never be true of us. God, our Father, has shown us such great kindness and gentle mercy. May we ever reach out to the lost in compassion and love to bring them gently to Jesus Christ. Jesus, "when He saw the multitudes, . . . was moved with compassion for them, because they were weary and scattered, like sheep having no shepherd" (Matt. 9:36).

Let me share these lines from an unknown poet:

Just to be tender, just to be true,
Just to be glad the whole day through,
Just to be merciful, just to be mild,
Just to be trustful as a child:
Just to be gentle and kind and sweet,
Just to be helpful with willing feet, . . .
Just to let love be our daily key,
That is God's will for you and me.

September 7

GOD HATES SIN

I acknowledged my sin to You,
and my iniquity I have not hidden.
PSALM 32:5

We live in an age when sin is winked at and where God is treated as one who is indulgent, softhearted, and understanding—tolerant of those who break His commandments. People today find it difficult to believe that God hates anything, much less sin. The image many people have of Him is of a rather senile old grandfather who shakes his head in amusement when his grandchildren misbehave.

But I will tell you that God has not forgotten about sin, though some may pretend it doesn't exist. God hates sin. Why? Because He loves us, and He knows the terrible devastation sin brings to us.

Sin is like a deadly cancer, inexorably bringing suffering and death in its wake. Left unforgiven, sin also sends men and women into a timeless eternity apart from God—into hell. God hates sin, because He hates what it does to us! Confess your sin today. Don't wait. Receive God's forgiveness and restoration so that you might be of use to Him and enjoy His love forever.

September 8

COMPLETE CONSECRATION

Whoever desires to come after Me, let him deny himself.
MARK 8:34

Today Christ is calling Christians to cleansing—to dedication—to consecration—to full surrender. If you are a Christian and have been suffering defeat or have been living outside the will of God, I beg you to surrender every area of your life to Christ.

Only surrendered Christians will make an impact on our world. The world does not need any more lukewarm Christians, or lazy Christians, or quarrelsome Christians, or doubting Christians, or prideful Christians. The Bible says, "a double minded man is unstable in all his ways" (James 1:8, KJV). What keeps you from a full surrender of your life to the King of kings and the Lord of lords?

Your response will make the difference between success and failure in your spiritual life. It will make the difference between your needing help and being able to help others. It will revolutionize your habits, your prayer life, your Bible reading, your giving, your testimony, and your church relationship. This is the Christian's hour of decision!

September 9

PEACE IN THE STORM

May the God of hope fill you with all joy and peace.
ROMANS 15:13

A wonderful old hymn says, "He gives us peace in the midst of a storm."

In life we face all kinds of storms. We usually think of the personal "storms" that come our way—financial worries, problems in our marriage or family, illness, the betrayal of a friend, and so forth. But we face other kinds of storms that threaten to engulf us also: storms of materialism, storms of secularism, storms of moral degeneracy, storms of injustice, terrorism, and war.

Do you remember the violent storm that came upon Jesus and His disciples one night on the Sea of Galilee? His disciples grew panicky—but Jesus stayed fast asleep. He was at peace because He knew God was in control. He was at peace also because He was sovereign over the storm, and He knew it would vanish at His Word: "Peace, be still!" (Mark 4:39).

His Word still calms the turmoil in our lives. Is some storm making you fearful today? Stay close to Jesus, for His Word brings peace.

September 10

REACH FOR HIS HAND

The Lord, He is the One who goes
before you. He will be with you.
DEUTERONOMY 31:8

Once many years ago when I was going through a dark period I prayed and prayed, but the heavens seemed to be brass. I felt as though God had disappeared and that I was alone with my trial and burden. It was a dark night for my soul.

I wrote my mother about the experience and will never forget her reply: "Son, there are many times when God withdraws to test your faith. He wants you to trust Him in the darkness. Now, Son, reach up by faith in the fog and you will find that His hand will be there." In tears I knelt by my bed and experienced an overwhelming sense of God's presence.

Whether or not we feel God's presence when our way seems dark, by faith we know He is there. You can stake your life on His promise: "I will never leave you nor forsake you" (Heb. 13:5).

September 11

THINGS THAT CANNOT BE SHAKEN

We are receiving a kingdom which cannot be shaken.
HEBREWS 12:28

This date of September 11 will be engraved on the memories of people everywhere for generations to come. On that terrible day when terrorists commandeered several passenger planes and killed thousands of innocent people in New York and Washington, we began to realize the true depths of evil in the human heart, and the uncertainty and fragility of life itself.

What lessons would God teach us from such an appalling tragedy? I confess I don't know the full answer. Many people, I know, for the first time faced the shallowness and emptiness of their lives, and turned to God as a result. Millions came together to pray.

But one lesson God would teach us all is this: Our only lasting hope is in Him. Life has always been uncertain; September 11 only made it clearer. Where will you turn for your security? Put your life in Christ's hands, for only He offers us "a kingdom which cannot be shaken."

September 12

ANGELS WATCHING

We should live soberly, righteously,
and godly in the present age.
TITUS 2:12

God's command to live righteous and godly lives should sober us, for the Bible tells us that our lives are Heaven's primary concern. Paul said, "I solemnly charge you in the presence of God and of Christ Jesus and of the chosen angels, that you guard and keep [these rules]" (1 Tim. 5:21, AB).

Think of it: Even the angels of Heaven are constantly watching how we live as Christians! Is it merely curiosity on their part, idly wondering if we will fail or prove faithful? No. They know the hour is urgent and that what we do is important. Eternal issues are at stake, and we are in the midst of a cosmic struggle.

Don't think it doesn't matter how you live; it does! It matters to God, and it matters to His holy angels. It also matters to those around you. Jesus said, "Let your light so shine before men, that they may see your good works and glorify your Father in heaven" (Matt. 5:16).

September 13

ABUNDANT PARDON

*Blessed is he whose transgression
is forgiven, whose sin is covered.*
PSALM 32:1

The story is told about a sensitive boy in the eighteenth century who joined the British Army, but when the shots began to fly, he deserted.

Years later he became a great astronomer, even discovering a new planet. King George sent for him. He came, fearful the king would order his execution for being a deserter. But he was given an envelope—and inside was a royal pardon. The king said, "Now we can talk, and you shall come up and live at Windsor Castle." He was Sir William Herschel.

Herschel was guilty and deserved condemnation. But King George had mercy on him, and even made him a member of the royal household.

This is what God promises us. We are guilty and helpless. But God loves us, and "Not by works of righteousness which we have done, but according to his mercy he saved us" (Titus 3:5, NIV). Never forget: "God did not send His Son into the world to condemn the world, but that the world through Him might be saved" (John 3:17).

THE PROPER PROPORTION

Do not love the world or the things in the world.
1 JOHN 2:15

Christians are warned not to love the world—but what is worldliness?

Some have misunderstood it.

Worldliness is an attitude, a spirit, an atmosphere that permeates the whole of human society. It is an attitude that puts self first and ignores God and His commandments. Its horizon is this present world, and it never gives a thought to God or to eternity. It exhibits itself in a thousand different ways—in habits, in selfish pleasures, in a grasping for material things, in driving ambition, in exalting oneself at the expense of others.

We must avoid everything God has labeled sinful; of that there can be no doubt. But some elements of daily life aren't necessarily sinful in themselves; they only become sinful if they are abused. Pleasure isn't always wrong—unless it is abused. Ambition is an essential part of true character—but if abused it can destroy us.

Be on guard, lest a spirit of worldliness creep into your life. The Bible warns, "Do not love the world, or the things in the world."

September 15

GOD VALUES FAITH

How precious also are Your thoughts to me,
O God! How great is the sum of them.
PSALM 139:17

How happy would a parent be if his child constantly questioned him whether his needs would be met? The parent would feel frustrated and sad, perhaps even angry that the child did not trust him.

The Bible has scores of references telling us how much it pleases God for us to trust Him for every need. The Roman soldier expressed great faith when he told Jesus just to "say the word" and his servant would be healed. Jesus told His disciples, "Look at the birds . . . they neither sow nor reap nor gather into barns; yet your heavenly Father feeds them. Are you not of more value than they?" (Matt. 6:26).

God values our trust in Him above every other character quality. And how do we develop trust? By spending time in God's presence, through prayer, worship, and reading His Word. We develop it also as we step out in faith, and discover He really can be trusted. Are you trusting Him for every need in your life?

September 16

KEPT BY THE SPIRIT

We know that He abides in us,
by the Spirit whom He has given us.
1 JOHN 3:24

A boat doesn't sink because it is in the water; it sinks because the water gets into it.

In the same way, Christians don't fail to live as they should because they are in the world; they fail because the world has gotten into them. We don't fail to produce the fruit of the Holy Spirit because we live in a sea of corruption; we fail because the sea of corruption has gotten into us.

It can happen almost without our realizing it. At one time we were dedicated to Christ, surrendered to the will of God. But little by little the chilling waters of the world crept in. We became preoccupied with the things of this world rather than the things of Christ.

Most ocean-going ships have pumps running constantly, sucking out any water that might have leaked into the hull. Similarly, we need to keep the "pumps" of repentance running. We need to plug the holes with the truth of God's Word. Don't let the world sink your ship!

September 17

PERFECT PEACE

May the God of hope fill you with all joy and peace.
ROMANS 15:13

I know that modern living taxes the faith of the greatest Christians, but none of us should doubt the ability of God to give us grace sufficient for our trials, even amid the stresses of this new century. The Christian is to trust quietly that God is still on the throne. He is a sovereign God, working out things according to His own plan.

Some section hands on a British railroad found a thrush's nest under the rail and the hen peacefully sitting on the eggs, undisturbed by the roar of the fast trains above and around her. What a picture of perfect trust! The Bible says, "You will keep him in perfect peace, whose mind is stayed on You" (Isa. 26:3).

Believe me, God's grace is more than adequate for these times. Even as I grow older, I am learning, day by day, to keep my mind centered on Christ. When we do, the worries and anxieties and concerns of the world pass away and nothing but "perfect peace" is left in the human heart.

September 18

PRAY WITHOUT CEASING

Men always ought to pray and not lose heart.
LUKE 18:1

A prayer does not have to be eloquent or contain the language and terms of a theologian. In fact, sometimes our simplest, most heartfelt prayers are the most pleasing to God.

When you made your decision for Christ, you became a child of God, adopted by Him into His family forever. Now you have the wonderful privilege of coming directly into His presence and addressing God as your Father. In the beginning you may not be fluent, but it's important to begin. My wife has a notebook she has kept of our children as they were beginning to talk. She treasures these first attempts, mistakes and all. She said, "I wouldn't take anything for that book."

When Paul said we should "pray without ceasing" (1 Thess. 5:17) he chose a term used in his day to describe a persistent cough. Repeatedly, throughout our day, we should be turning quickly to God to praise and thank Him, and to ask for His help. God is interested in everything we do, and nothing is too great or too insignificant to share with Him.

September 19

CHRIST IS COMING AGAIN

Looking for the blessed hope and glorious appearing of our ... Savior Jesus Christ.
TITUS 2:13

One of the best ways to get rid of discouragement is to remember that Christ is coming again. What is happening in your life right now is not going to last forever!

The most thrilling, glorious truth in all the world is the second coming of Jesus Christ. When we look about today and see pessimism on every side, we should remember the Bible is the only book in the world that reliably predicts the future. The Bible is more modern than tomorrow's newspaper. It says the consummation of all things shall be the coming again of Jesus Christ to this earth.

This truth gives us hope—but it should also sober us and make us more diligent. After all, we do not know when Christ will return. Jesus Himself said, "Of that day and hour no one knows, not even the angels of heaven, but My Father only" (Matt. 24:36). Believing in the return of Christ doesn't make us less concerned about this world; it makes us more concerned, because we know time may be short. *Now* is the time to live for Christ and witness for Him.

September 20

THE STAFF OF LIFE

Your word I have hidden in my heart,
that I might not sin against you.
PSALM 119:11

The Bible isn't just another great book. It is God's Word, given by God to tell us about Himself. Peter declared, "We did not follow cunningly devised fables . . . for prophecy never came by the will of man, but holy men of God spoke as they were moved by the Holy Spirit" (2 Pet. 1:16, 21). Paul stressed, "All Scripture is given by inspiration of God, and is profitable for doctrine, for reproof, for correction, for instruction in righteousness" (2 Tim. 3:16).

I have known many outstanding leaders who made the Bible their guide. Businessman Herbert J. Taylor, former president of Rotary International, told me he began each day by reading the Sermon on the Mount aloud.

Let the Bible be your firm foundation. Let it be the staff of life that nourishes your soul. Let it be the sword of the Spirit that cuts away sin. Many years ago I heard these words: "Sin will keep you from God's Word—or God's Word will keep you from sin!"

September 21

GOD OF ALL COMFORT

Because he ... suffered when he was tempted,
he is able to help those who are being tempted.
HEBREWS 2:18, NIV

Once when I was in my latter teens I was in love with a girl. It might have been puppy love, but it was real to me, the "puppy"! We became tentatively engaged to be married, even though we were both much too young. However, she felt that the Lord was leading her to another young man—one of my best friends.

I suffered a broken heart, and I remember going to a clergyman friend of mine to seek his help. He turned me to 2 Corinthians 1:3-4: "Blessed be the God and Father of our Lord Jesus Christ ... who comforts us in all our tribulation, that we may be able to comfort those who are in any trouble, with the comfort with which we ourselves are comforted by God."

From those words of the apostle I gained comfort. But there is more to it than that. This passage from Paul suggests a new insight into suffering. Briefly put, it is this: Not only are we comforted in our trials, but our trials can equip us to comfort others. Has God taught you something through your trials that could help someone else today?

SEARCHING FOR HOPE

In the world you will have tribulation; but be
of good cheer, I have overcome the world.
JOHN 16:33

Once when I referred to the future that God is planning, a university student asked me, "Isn't this a form of escapism?" I said, "In a sense, yes; and before the devil gets through with this world, we are all going to be looking for exit signs!"

As Christians we look beyond this world to God's promise of "new heavens and a new earth in which righteousness dwells" (2 Pet. 3:13). But in the meantime, the world remains mired in the same heartaches and injustices it has suffered since the Fall—and Jesus said we shouldn't be surprised: "In the world you will have tribulation."

Some people mistakenly think if they become Christians, God will take away all their problems. It just isn't so. Sin still dwells within us, and Satan is still at work.

But that isn't the full story! Jesus added, "But be of good cheer, I have overcome the world." Notice: He not only *will* overcome the world—He already *has!*

September 23

GOD'S WORD

Desire the pure milk of the word,
that you may grow thereby.
1 PETER 2:2

Just as our bodies need food, so our souls need spiritual food. Without it we become malnourished and weak, susceptible to every temptation and unable to do the work God calls us to do.

Where do we find this spiritual food? In the Bible, the Word of God. The Bible reveals Christ, the Bread of Life and the Water of Life. If we fail to partake of this spiritual nourishment, we will lose our spiritual vitality.

Some parts of our world do not enjoy the freedom we have to read the Bible. But most of us cannot hide behind that excuse. The problem for most of us is not *getting* a Bible, but *using* a Bible—actually picking it up and reading it.

Don't be content to skim through a chapter, merely to satisfy your conscience or because of some long-established habit. Rather, read it as if your life depended on it. Meditate on it, memorize it, hide it in your heart so it permeates your whole being. A small portion well digested is of far greater spiritual value than a lengthy passage scanned hurriedly.

September 24

GOD'S REVELATION

Forever, O Lord, Your word is settled in heaven.
PSALM 119:89

What does *revelation* mean? It means that something that has been hidden is now made known. If it isn't revealed, it remains hidden.

Some people see God that way—hidden and unknown. Such a view assumes God doesn't want to be known—or even that God is incapable of being known because "God" is just a vague impersonal force, like gravity.

But God *has* revealed Himself. He is not hidden! He has spoken to us, and if we will listen, we can not only discover what He is like, but we can come to know Him in a personal way.

God has two textbooks. One is the "textbook" of nature. By looking at the world, we can learn something about its Creator.

The other is the "textbook" of revelation, the Bible. It is more than an ancient record of events; it is God's Word, given to us by the inspiration of the Holy Spirit to guide our lives. God has spoken—and He still speaks. Are you listening?

September 25

Treasure that Lasts

Lay up for yourselves treasures in heaven.
Matthew 6:20

Some time ago two old friends were dying. One was rich, and the other poor. The rich man was outside of Christ, but the poor man was a strong believer. One day the rich man was talking to another of his friends. "When I die," he said, "I shall have to leave my riches. When he dies, he will go to his riches."

Thus in just a couple of sentences the rich man summed up the contrast between them. The man worth everything, in reality, had nothing; the man with nothing, in reality, had everything.

These two men were a vivid illustration of what Jesus said to His disciples: "Do not lay up for yourselves treasures on earth . . . but lay up for yourselves treasures in heaven. . . . For where your treasure is, there your heart will be also" (Matt. 6:19–21).

Does that mean we must renounce everything we own? No, not unless God clearly commands us to do so. But it does mean we commit everything we have—including our lives—to Christ, and put His will above everything else.

September 26

FAITH IN GOD

Faith is the substance of things hoped for.
HEBREWS 11:1

Faith must have an object. We don't simply have faith; we have faith *in* something or someone. Faith in "faith" is meaningless.

For the Christian there is only one object for faith: the living God. Anything less is insubstantial, unreal, even deceptive. Our faith is in the God who created this world and came down to earth in the person of His Son, Jesus Christ. We put our faith in Christ because He alone is the Savior. The Bible says, "Through Him [you] believe in God, who raised Him from the dead and gave Him glory, so that your faith and hope are in God" (1 Pet. 1:21).

People today put their faith in all kinds of ideas and beliefs, from astrology and alleged "spirit guides" to science and humanism. But only Christ reveals God to us, and only He can bridge the gap between us and God—a gap caused by sin. Do not be deceived or misled. Only Christ is worthy of your faith.

September 27

OUR GREAT ASSURANCE

*Let us draw near with a true heart
in full assurance of faith.*
HEBREWS 10:22

Disregard your feelings when you come to
Christ. You aren't saved by your feelings; you
are saved by Christ. Feelings come and go, but
Christ remains.

Only the facts matter—the fact that Jesus Christ
died for your sins and rose again; the fact that if you
have committed your life to Him, He has promised
to forgive you and save you. The Bible says, "God has
given us eternal life, and this life is in His Son. He who
has the Son has life" (1 John 5:11–12).

That is God's promise to you—and He cannot lie.
Your feelings will lie to you—and Satan may even use
them to convince you God has abandoned you or that
you have lost your salvation. But remember: "There
is no truth in him. When he lies, he speaks his native
language, for he is a liar and the father of lies"
(John 8:44, NIV).

How wonderful to know our faith is based on God's
truth, and not our feelings!

September 28

TO DIE IS GAIN

For to me, to live is Christ and to die is gain.
PHILIPPIANS 1:21, NIV

Most of us know what it means to be stunned by the sudden passing of a dedicated friend, a godly pastor, a devout missionary, or a saintly mother. We have stood at the open grave with hot tears running down our cheeks and have asked in utter bewilderment, "Why, O God, why?" We know the impact these people made, and we can't help but think of the good they might have continued to do, had they lived longer.

The death of the righteous is no accident. Do you think that God—whose watchful vigil notes the sparrow's fall and who knows the number of hairs on our heads—would turn His back on one of His children in the hour of peril? With Him there are no accidents, no tragedies, and no catastrophes as far as His children are concerned.

It was Sir Walter Scott who asked, "Is death the last sleep? No, it is the final awakening." That is true for every believer in Christ. Even when grief overwhelms us or confusion assails us, we still can trust God's all-knowing love.

September 29

SAFE AND SECURE

*He became the author of eternal
salvation to all who obey Him.*
HEBREWS 5:9

With the exception of Jesus, no one in the Bible probably endured more scorn than Noah. Told to build an ark to escape God's judgment, we read that "Noah did; according to all that God commanded him" (Gen. 6:22).

Can you imagine what his neighbors said? Can you picture them shaking their heads and laughing, calling him a fool and murmuring he must be out of his mind? Can you envision them angrily rejecting his warnings of coming judgment and returning to their idolatrous ways (for 2 Pet. 2:5 calls Noah "a preacher of righteousness")?

But when the flood came, only Noah and his family were saved. For those who scorned his pleas, it was too late.

You and I are called to proclaim a message that often seems foolishness to an unbelieving world—the message of the Cross. Will everyone accept it? No. Will some mock us? Yes. But never stop sharing the Gospel, for it is still "the power of God that brings salvation to everyone who believes" (Rom. 1:16, NIV).

September 30

DISPEL DISCOURAGEMENT

Wait on the Lord; be of good courage,
and He shall strengthen your heart.
PSALM 27:14

The root of discouragement is unbelief. Perhaps you are discouraged because you think you aren't making enough money (and you aren't convinced God can supply your needs). Or you are frustrated in your job (and you refuse to believe God can help you be content). Or maybe you are worried about health problems (and you don't even stop to consider that your life is in God's hands).

Discouragement is a large cloud that, like all clouds, obscures the warmth and joy of the sun. In the case of spiritual discouragement, the Son of God, the Lord Jesus, is eclipsed in our lives. Discouragement is Satan's device to thwart the work of God in our lives. Discouragement blinds our eyes to the mercy of God and makes us perceive only the unfavorable circumstances.

There is only one way to dispel discouragement, and it is not in our own strength or ingenuity. It is to turn in faith to God, believing that He loves us and is in control of the future. The Bible says, "Wait on the LORD . . . and He shall strengthen your heart."

October

Pray that God will give you boldness as you share your faith day by day and especially during the culmination of My Hope *with Billy Graham next month.*

October 1

TRIUMPH OVER TRAGEDY

*Every good gift and every perfect gift is from above,
and comes down from the Father of lights.*
JAMES 1:17

The key to understanding tragedy is to understand its source. Death and pain and every other tragedy came into this world because of sin. When Adam and Eve sinned in the Garden of Eden, they weren't just doing something God had told them not to do. It was a blatant, open act of rebellion—in thought, word, and deed—against the God who had made them and had supplied their every need. It was saying God was a liar and believing Satan instead. It was yielding to the temptation to "be like God" (Gen. 3:5).

Every graveyard, every hospital, every prison, every courtroom is a witness to the terrible legacy of that rebellion. No, I don't fully understand why God allows evil to happen. But evil happens because we live in an evil world. Never underestimate the devastating effects of sin.

What was sin's greatest tragedy? It was the Cross—for had it not been for sin, Jesus would never have had to die. But Christ triumphed over tragedy—and so can we, because of Him.

October 2

POOR IN SPIRIT

Where your treasure is, there your heart will be also.
MATTHEW 6:21

One of the hardest truths for some people to accept is that there is absolutely nothing they can do to win their salvation.

No matter how generous . . . how honest . . . how compassionate they are—it is never enough. God is holy, and His standard is perfection. If we think we are good enough, it simply proves our pride.

Only when we see ourselves as God sees us—sinners, guilty before Him—will we realize our need of a Savior. C. H. Spurgeon said, "The first link between my soul and Christ is not my goodness but my badness, not my merit but my misery, not my riches but my need."

But the amazing thing is this: In spite of our sin, God still loves us. He loves us so much that Christ died on the cross for us. All we can do is *believe* and *receive*—*believe* Christ died for us and by faith *receive* Him into our lives. No, you can't win your salvation—but Christ has won it for you!

October 3

ANSWERED PRAYER

Let us ... come boldly to the throne of grace, that we may obtain mercy.
HEBREWS 4:16

Frequently people say to me, "God answered my prayer!" Usually they mean God granted them whatever they had requested, either for themselves or for others.

God *always* answers the prayers of His children—but His answer isn't always "Yes." Sometimes His answer is "No," or "Wait"—and they are answers just as much as "Yes."

Think of Paul, pleading with God to remove his "thorn in the flesh" (probably a painful illness). But God's answer was "No" (see 2 Cor. 12:7–10). God had something better—a path leading him into deeper dependence on God and His grace. Or think of Jesus, praying as He faced the agony of the Cross: "If it is possible, let this cup pass from Me" (Matt. 26:39). But God's answer was "No"—because there was no other way for our salvation to be won.

God knows far better than we do what is best for us. Thank God even when He says "No" or "Wait." His answer is always perfect.

October 4

GOD'S PLANS ARE BEST

As for God, His way is perfect.

PSALM 18:30

Things didn't always work out the way Paul planned.

Expecting to preach in Asia Minor, "they were forbidden by the Holy Spirit" (Acts 16:6). Looking forward to instructing the new converts in Philippi, Paul and his companion instead found themselves thrown into prison (see Acts 16:11 ff.). Encouraged by the response to the Gospel in Thessalonica, he was suddenly assailed by a mob and accused of having "turned the world upside down" (Acts 17:6). As a result he was forced to flee.

But in every instance God was in control! Paul was forbidden to preach in Asia Minor—because God was opening the door to Europe. Paul found himself in jail—and as a result the Philippian jailer and his family were converted. Paul had to flee Thessalonica—and Berea, the next town, "received the word with all readiness" (Acts 17:11).

Things don't always work out the way we plan. But if we commit our way to Christ and walk in obedience to Him, we discover His plans are always better.

October 5

MATERIALISM

You cannot serve God and mammon.
LUKE 16:13

The Bible strictly forbids idolatry. One of the Ten Commandments declares, "You shall not make for yourself a carved image; . . . you shall not bow down to them nor serve them" (Exod. 20:4–5).

But almost anything can become an "idol"— something we worship and serve in place of God. It might be success, or pleasure, or possessions, or money, or anything else we let control our lives. They aren't necessarily wrong in themselves, but they become "idols" when we make them the most important things in life.

The Bible rejects idols for at least two reasons. First, idols are false. They cannot save us or change our lives for the better. Second, idols cut us off from God. We substitute them for God—and as a result, we turn our backs on Him and never come to know Him and love Him as we should.

Has any "idol" taken God's rightful place in your life? Don't let it happen. God has commanded, "You shall have no other gods before Me" (Exod. 20:3).

October 6

STRANGERS IN THE WORLD

I urge you, as foreigners and exiles,
to abstain from sinful desires.
1 PETER 2:11, NIV

Aliens from other countries are rarely shown the "welcome mat." They are often accepted reluctantly or with a tongue-in-cheek attitude. They may even find themselves victims of discrimination, rejection, or intolerance.

The Bible says that we are "aliens and strangers in the world." Our citizenship is in Heaven and there is our real home. As long as we live on this earth, we don't quite fit in. Our customs are different, our goals are different, our ways of living are different, our concerns are different.

And as Christ's followers (instead of followers of this world), we may find ourselves scorned, rejected, or even persecuted. If so, we shouldn't be surprised. Jesus warned, "If they persecuted Me, they will also persecute you" (John 15:20).

But never forget: You are a citizen of the Kingdom of God. And someday you will be Home!

October 7

YIELDED TO GOD

*Know ye not, that to whom ye yield yourselves
servants to obey, his servants ye are ... ?*
ROMANS 6:16, KJV

O f Eric Liddell, the missionary and great runner
whose story is told in the film *Chariots of
Fire,* someone has said, he was "ridiculously
humble in victory, utterly generous in defeat." That's
a good definition of what it means to be meek. Eric
Liddell was fiercely competitive, determined to use his
God-given abilities to the fullest. But his meekness,
kindness, and gentle spirit won the admiration even
of those he defeated.

Meekness involves being yielded. The word *yield*
has two meanings. The first is negative, and the second
is positive. On one hand it means "to relinquish, to
abandon"; on the other hand, it also means "to give."
This is in line with Jesus' words: "He who loses [or
abandons] his life ... will find it" (Matt. 10:39).

Those who submit to the will of God do not fight
back at life. They learn the secret of yielding—of
relinquishing and abandoning—their own lives and
wills to Christ. And then He gives back to them a life
that is far richer and fuller than anything they could
ever have imagined.

October 8

GOD'S MESSAGE

He who hears My word, and believes
Him who sent Me, has eternal life.
JOHN 5:24, NASB

I know little about nuclear fission or uranium and other elements used in making nuclear explosives. Yet I believe in the atomic bomb, and so do you. But how can we believe that it exists, if we don't understand it or have any scientific knowledge about the way it works?

The answer is obvious. Others understand nuclear fission even if we don't, and others have seen what happens when a nuclear reaction takes place, even if we haven't. We read what they say, and we accept it as the evidence of reliable witnesses.

I spend much of my time perusing the pages of a book—the Bible. In it I discover that centuries ago God acted and spoke, and reliable witnesses have written it down. God even guided them as they wrote, so that now I read the very words of God Himself.

I may not understand everything there is to know about God—but I know Him and trust Him, because I read of Him in the Bible. Most of all, I know He came down to this earth in the person of His Son, and "grace and truth came by Jesus Christ" (John 1:17).

October 9

Surrounded with Song

You shall surround me with songs of deliverance.
Psalm 32:7

Someone has said that when faith is strong, troubles become trifles.

That doesn't mean our troubles aren't real, or that we act as if they didn't exist. God takes them seriously—so seriously that He sent Jesus Christ into the world to deal with their root cause, which is sin.

But just as Jesus triumphed over death, so He helps us triumph over trouble. Even in the midst of troubles, the Bible says, "I will turn their mourning to joy" (Jer. 31:13).

How does it happen? By looking in faith to God. He has not abandoned us, and He has plans for our future. He can even give us an optimistic spirit—somewhat like the Englishman I heard about during World War II who stood looking at the deep hole in the ground where his bombed-out home had once stood. "I always did want a basement, I did," he said. "Now I can jolly well build another house like I always wanted!"

October 10

THE CLOUDS OF LIFE

*The Lord went before them by day
in a pillar of cloud to lead the way.*
EXODUS 13:21

Clouds will come. They are part of life. But by God's grace we need not be depressed by them. Just as clouds can protect us from the brightness of the sun, life's clouds can reveal the glory of God, and from their lofty height God speaks to us.

Like the children of Israel, we are travelers to the Promised Land. As they traveled through the wilderness, the Bible says, "The LORD went before them by day in a pillar of cloud to lead the way."

Perhaps like them, you are passing through a wilderness right now. It may be the wilderness of a broken marriage, or a financial reversal, or a major disappointment, or a threatening illness. It may even be a wilderness of doubt or sin.

But God is with you in the wilderness, and He goes before you to encourage and guide you. He brought the children of Israel through the wilderness—and He will bring you through it as well, as you look in faith to Him. Never forget: "He is the living God, and steadfast forever" (Dan. 6:26).

October 11

REDEEMED BY LOVE

You were redeemed . . . with the precious blood of Christ.
1 PETER 1:18–19, NIV

The word *redeem* means to "buy back"—to recover by paying a price. The word *redeemed* can be illustrated from the ancient world by the position of a slave who had been captured in battle or enticed into serving one who was not his legal master. His real master, however, intent on recovering his slave's service and love, would buy him back—redeem him from the enemy—at great personal cost.

That is what God did for us. Captured by Satan and enticed into his service, we were slaves of sin, without any hope of deliverance. But God still loved us, and He was determined to restore us to His household. By His death on the Cross, Jesus paid the price for our deliverance, a price far greater than our true value. He did it solely because He loved us. Now we have been redeemed!

October 12

DETERMINED DISCIPLES

If you abide in My word, you are My disciples indeed.
JOHN 8:31

A disciple in Jesus' time was someone who followed a teacher or philosopher. A disciple was both a learner and a follower—believing the teacher's message and then putting it into practice.

Jesus gave the word *disciple* added meaning, however, because His disciples also went out to tell others about Him. A disciple of Jesus, therefore, is someone who has committed his or her life to Jesus, and seeks each day to *learn*, to *follow*, and to *share* Him with others. Does this describe you?

No, the first disciples weren't perfect, and neither are we. Like them, we need to learn more and follow more, and share more. But all of us who belong to Christ are called to be disciples. Unlike the original disciples, we can't physically spend time with Jesus, but we can learn from Him by reading His Word. We can follow Him by obeying His will. And we can share Him with a world that desperately needs to be saved.

October 13

AN ALTERED ATTITUDE

Return to the Lord your God, for
He is gracious and merciful.
JOEL 2:13

From time to time I have had people pour out their heart to me because their sins had been discovered and they were in serious trouble. They wept bitterly because they had devastated their marriage or ruined their reputation.

But later someone would tell me they were back in the same situation. They had not learned from their experience, and seemed determined to bring even more chaos into their lives.

What was the problem? The problem was lack of repentance. Their tears were tears of self-pity—but not of repentance. True repentance is a turning *from* sin—a conscious, deliberate decision to leave sin behind—and a conscious turning *to* God, with a commitment to follow His will.

Repentance is only one part of our response to Christ (and even the strength to repent comes from God). But it is an essential part, for without it we cannot claim Christ is our Lord. The Bible says, "Godly sorrow brings repentance that leads to salvation and leaves no regret" (2 Cor. 7:10, NIV).

Triumph Through Trust

Neither death nor life, . . . nor things present nor things to come, . . . shall be able to separate us from the love of God.

ROMANS 8:38–39

There are two ways to respond to adversity: discouragement or trust.

The problem with giving in to discouragement is that it only makes things worse, for with it may come bitterness, anger, jealousy, revenge, and so forth. We may even try to escape through drugs or alcohol. But do *any* of these solve the problem? No!

God has a better way—the way of trust. Sometimes He may show us that we were in the wrong. When that is the case, we need to confess it, repent, and seek His forgiveness. Sometimes, however, we can only accept what is happening and ask God to help us endure it and triumph over it.

One of the best ways to overcome adversity, I've found, is to praise God right in the middle of the turmoil. Turning to God's Word will also encourage us; many of the Psalms, for example, were written in the midst of suffering and adversity. Follow the Psalmist's example: "Bless the LORD, O my soul, and forget not all His benefits" (Ps. 103:2).

October 15

AN UPSIDE-DOWN WORLD

God is not ashamed to be called their God.
HEBREWS 11:16

We live in an upside-down world. People hate when they should love, quarrel when they should be friendly, fight when they should be peaceful, wound when they should heal, steal when they should share, do wrong when they should do right.

I once saw a toy clown with a weight in its head. No matter how it was placed, it invariably assumed an upside-down position. It could be placed on its feet or on its side and when let go it flipped back on its head.

The clown illustrates why the disciples seemed to be misfits to the world. To an upside-down man, a right-side-up man seems upside down. To the nonbeliever, the true Christian is an oddity and an abnormality.

Yet this isn't the whole picture, for all around us are people who sense something is wrong with their topsy-turvy lives, and they yearn to be right side up. Will you pray for them and ask God to help you point them to life's only solid foundation—Jesus Christ?

October 16

HOPE FROM GOD'S WORD

*The grass withers, the flower fades, but
the word of our God stands forever.*

ISAIAH 40:8

A missionary in China who was imprisoned by the Japanese during World War II, managed to take a forbidden Gospel of John with her into prison. She carefully hid it, and each night when she went to bed, she pulled the covers over her head and memorized one verse. She did this until the day she was freed.

When the prisoners were released, most of them shuffled out, but the missionary was so chipper someone said she must have been brainwashed. A *Life* magazine reporter who had interviewed her said, "She's been brainwashed for sure. God washed her brain."

I urge you not only to read God's Word but to memorize it. You may find it hard at first, but as you repeat a verse or a group of verses over and over to yourself, you will find they begin to take root in your soul. The Psalmist declared, "Your word I have hidden in my heart, that I might not sin against You" (Ps. 119:11). Then when adversity or troubles arise, those verses will come back and give you hope.

Is God's Word stored up in your heart and mind for the future?

October 17

LOVE AND MARRIAGE

He who loves his wife loves himself.
EPHESIANS 5:28

There are three elements to a successful marriage. The first is love—not just an emotional feeling or a physical attraction, but a deep commitment to put the other person first.

The apostle Paul defined love beautifully in 1 Corinthians 13. Read it and you will know how God defines love. Men are to love their wives as Christ loved the Church. What woman wouldn't respond to such a selfless expression of love?

Maturity is the second ingredient in a successful marriage. Too many are getting a divorce at the first sign of trouble. Maturity means a willingness to act responsibly and not take the easy way out.

Third, faith must be an ingredient for a marriage to be successful. Marriage is difficult enough these days with all of life's pressures, but without Christ at the center of a marriage and a home, it becomes even more difficult. It takes three to make a great marriage: you, your spouse, and Christ. I have seldom seen a marriage fail when the husband and wife pray and worship God together.

GOD WANTS OUR FELLOWSHIP

Come near to God and he will come near to you.
JAMES 4:8, NIV

What a blessed promise and provision this is! It means each of us can come close to God, with the assurance He will come close to us—so close that we become conscious of His presence. This is the greatest experience we can know.

But for most of us this isn't easy. Life presents us with too many distractions, and the last thing we have time for is to be alone with God. Children, work, television, the Internet, even church activities drain away our time.

Maybe you will have to readjust your priorities. Maybe you will have to say "No" to certain activities or demands. Whatever it takes, make time to be alone with God.

Remember: He *wants* your fellowship, and He has done everything possible to make it a reality. He has forgiven your sins, at the cost of His own dear Son. He has given you His Word, and the priceless privilege of prayer and worship.

He *will* come near to you, if you will come near to Him.

October 19

TEACHER AND GUIDE

When He, the Spirit of truth, has come,
He will guide you into all truth.
JOHN 16:13

The moment you receive Jesus Christ as Savior and Lord, the Holy Spirit takes up residence in your heart. Right now He lives within you! The Bible says, "If anyone does not have the Spirit of Christ, he is not His" (Rom. 8:9).

The Holy Spirit helps us in life's struggles, and we must never forget that. But the Holy Spirit also plays two other important roles we must not overlook.

First, He convicts us of sin. The Bible says, "He will convict the world of sin, and of righteousness, and of judgment" (John 16:8). While this verse focuses on His convicting power among unbelievers, the Holy Spirit also convicts believers when we sin.

The second role of the Holy Spirit is as Teacher. The Bible says, "He will guide you into all truth." Just as surely as the Holy Spirit inspired the writers of the Bible, so He will instruct us as we meditate on God's Word.

Are you a willing student of the Holy Spirit?

MOVED WITH COMPASSION

You, O Lord, are a God full of compassion . . .
abundant in mercy and truth.
PSALM 86:15

The word *compassion* comes from two Latin words meaning "to suffer with." What better picture to describe God's compassion for us? Suffering is the common lot of the human race. We see pictures on television of people ravaged by war or famine, and our hearts are touched (as they should be). But all around you are people who suffer in others ways: loneliness, fear, rejection, disability, grief, poverty, discrimination, addiction, or a multitude of other problems.

But God has compassion on us—He suffers with us. He knows what we are going through, and He cares. The greatest act of compassion in the history of the human race was the Cross, for there Christ suffered for us. He endured sin's penalty so we would not have to endure it ourselves.

Now He calls us to have compassion on others, for His sake—to suffer *with* them, and to point them to the One who suffered *for* them. The Bible says, "Be sympathetic, love as brothers, be compassionate and humble" (1 Pet. 3:8, NIV).

October 21

"Come Home"

*Our citizenship is in heaven, from which
we also eagerly wait for the Savior.*
Philippians 3:20

Once there was a widow and her son who lived
in a miserable attic. Years before, she had
married against her parents' wishes and had
gone with her husband to live in a foreign land.

He had proved irresponsible and unfaithful, and
after a few years he died without having made any
provision for her and the child. It was with the utmost
difficulty that she managed to scrape together the
bare necessities of life.

One day the postman knocked at the attic door. The
mother recognized the handwriting on the letter he
brought and with trembling fingers broke the seal.
There was a check and a slip of paper with just two
words: "Come home."

Someday a similar experience will be ours—an
experience shared by all who know Christ. We do
not know when the call will come. It may be when we
are in the midst of our work. It may be after weeks or
months of illness. But someday a loving hand will be
laid upon our shoulder and this brief message will be
given: "Come home."

October 22

IT WAS LOVE

I have loved you with an everlasting love;
therefore with lovingkindness I have drawn you.
JEREMIAH 31:3

M any people have difficulty believing God is a God of love. "How could He be," they ask, "when the world is filled with so much suffering and evil?" It is not an easy issue—but if you really want to know the reality of God's love, look at the Cross.

It was love, divine love, that made Christ endure the Cross, despising the shame.

It was love that restrained Him when He was falsely accused of blasphemy and led to Golgotha to die with common thieves. He raised not a hand against His enemies. It was love that kept Him from calling legions of angels to come to His defense.

It was love that made Him, in a moment of agonizing pain, pause and give hope to a repentant sinner who cried, "Lord, remember me when You come into Your kingdom" (Luke 23:42).

It was love that caused Jesus to lift His voice and pray, "Father, forgive them, for they do not know what they do" (Luke 23:34). Does God love us? Yes—and the proof is the Cross.

October 23

A CLEAR CONSCIENCE

The blood of Christ, ... [will] cleanse our consciences.
HEBREWS 9:14, NIV

Each of us has a conscience that sits as a judge over our every thought, word, and deed. It can be sensitive, undeveloped, or distorted, depending upon the way we have used or abused it.

The human conscience is defiled by sin, says the Bible—and that is one reason it is not a reliable guide by itself. Our conscience needs to be cleansed by the purifying work of the Holy Spirit, and honed and sharpened by the truth of the Word of God. Satan can even twist our consciences if they are not yielded to Christ and convince us that wrong is really right.

But in spite of its frailty, our conscience is still important, and God still uses it to warn us of danger. All of us have experienced the backlash of guilt after a transgression.

Is God speaking to you about something that is not right in your life? Something you may be doing—but you know dishonors Christ? Don't ignore that voice or think it doesn't matter. Face it, confess it, put it right, and never touch it again.

October 24

RESTING FAITH

The testing of your faith produces patience.
JAMES 1:3

Dwight L. Moody was fond of pointing out that there are three kinds of faith in Jesus Christ: *struggling faith,* which is like a man floundering and fearful in deep water; *clinging faith,* which is like a man hanging to the side of a boat; and *resting faith,* which finds a man safe inside the boat—strong and secure enough to reach out his hand to help someone else.

Notice each man had faith. Each knew the boat was his only hope. But only one had a *resting* faith. Only one had discovered he could actually be *in* the boat— where all he had to do was rest.

This is the kind of faith God wants us to have— a faith that trusts Him totally. But sometimes we discover its reality only after we have endured a struggling or clinging faith. Sometimes we only realize we can get *in* the boat when the storm rages and we cry out to God with new faith. Then our Savior graciously extends His hand and says, "Come to Me . . . and I will give you rest" (Matt. 11:28).

October 25

DOING GOD'S WILL

Doing the will of God from the heart.
EPHESIANS 6:6

We are admonished to seek out the will of the Lord. In Ephesians 5:17 we read, "Therefore do not be unwise, but understand what the will of the Lord is."

Some people, however, misunderstand the will of God. They think it must be a harsh, joyless thing, intended to make us miserable. But listen: God's will comes from God's love.

If you love someone, will you want to make him miserable? Will you go out of your way to punish him if he doesn't do exactly what you tell him to? No, of course not—not if you really love him.

The same is true with God. God loves you, and because He loves you, He cares what happens to you. He loves you too much to let you wander aimlessly through life, without meaning or purpose. The Bible says, "You will show me the path of life; in Your presence is fullness of joy" (Ps.16:11).

Covet God's will for your life more than anything else. To know God's will—and to do it—is life's greatest joy.

October 26

ONE SURE GUIDE

Your word is a lamp to my feet and a light to my path.
PSALM 119:105

As Christians, we have only one authority, one compass: the Word of God.

In the midst of a thousand different voices, all claiming their own authority and clamoring for our allegiance, only one Voice will tell us the truth. That Voice? The written Word of God, given to us by God to tell us what we are to believe and how we are to live. As the Psalmist said, "The entrance of Your words gives light" (Ps. 119:130).

In a letter to a friend, Abraham Lincoln said, "I am profitably engaged in reading the Bible. Take all of this Book upon reason that you can and the balance upon faith, and you will live and die a better man."

Coleridge said he believed the Bible to be the Word of God because, as he put it, "It finds me."

"If you want encouragement," John Bunyan wrote, "entertain the promises."

Martin Luther said, "In Scriptures, even the little daisy becomes a meadow."

The Bible is our one sure guide in an unsure world. Is it your guide?

October 27

THE ARK OF SALVATION

By faith Noah, . . . became an heir of the righteousness which comes by faith.
HEBREWS 11:7, RSV

The Bible warned the people of Noah's day, "My Spirit shall not strive with man forever" (Gen. 6:3). They laughed at Noah and mocked his words, and went about their usual business and their pleasures without ever dreaming he might be right. God was speaking—but they ignored Him. Eventually God's patience gave out—and by then it was too late.

Outside the ark men and women struggled for their lives, clutching at pieces of driftwood, until the pitiless hand of death reached up and drew them down beneath those cruel waves. All were lost. Every soul outside the ark perished. They had had their chance, but tossed it away.

You cannot come to Christ unless the Spirit of God brings you. But what if you ignore His warnings? Then you are in the gravest danger, for someday God will no longer be speaking to you. Then it will be too late. Come to Christ while there is still time. Christ, God's greater Ark, stands ready to welcome you to safety today.

Are you in the Ark?

October 28

GOD IS NEVER LATE

The Lord is your keeper; the Lord is your shade at your right hand.

PSALM 121:5

In order for a tree or any plant to grow and bear fruit, its seed must first be planted in the ground and die. In order for spiritual fruit to appear in our lives, we must first be planted in the Word of God and then die to self. In the face of chastening, adversity, discipline, and affliction, God's Word nourishes our lives and fruit begins to appear. But it doesn't happen overnight. It takes time and patience.

Joseph would never have been of use to God had he not been sold into slavery by brothers who hated him, and then wrongly accused by Potiphar, who put him in prison. Even after he had told Pharaoh's cupbearer he would be restored to the king's court and asked him to tell Pharaoh of his unjust imprisonment, Joseph had to wait two more years for release from prison.

As we wait upon the Lord, He may sometimes seem slow in coming to help us, but He never comes too late. His timing is always perfect.

October 29

Citizens of Heaven

Because I live, you will live also.
John 14:19

People spend billions of dollars every year on cosmetics, health spas, physical fitness machines, and concoctions claiming to make them live longer or slow down the aging process. But age will overtake even the most beautiful or physically fit people in the world, and eventually they will die—as will we.

But someday we who know Christ will have perfect bodies—bodies that will never age or experience pain. Someday our dead bodies will be "raised in glory" (1 Cor. 15:43), and we will be like Christ in His resurrection body.

Can I imagine what that will be like? Not fully. But I do know this: The resurrected body of Jesus is the pattern or design for our new bodies. "For our citizenship is in heaven, from which we also eagerly wait for the Savior, the Lord Jesus Christ, who will transform our lowly body that it may be conformed to His glorious body" (Phil. 3:20–21).

What a future we have in Christ!

October 30

Finding Fulfillment

Let your soul delight itself in abundance.
ISAIAH 55:2

When Satan tried to trap Jesus at the beginning of His ministry, he used the same temptations he uses today.

One trap was the lure of things. Jesus had fasted for forty days, and Satan tried to take advantage of His hunger by urging Him to use His supernatural power to turn stones into bread. But Jesus replied, "Man shall not live by bread alone, but by every word that proceeds from the mouth of God" (Matt. 4:4). Not from Satan's mouth, but from God's!

Bread is important—but it isn't all-important, as Satan was suggesting. Pleasure and recreation have their place—but they mustn't have first place. Money is necessary, but money must serve us; we are not to serve it.

Isaiah said, "Listen carefully to Me . . . and let your soul delight itself in abundance" (Isa. 55:2). Yes, delight in abundance—the abundance God gives you, both material and spiritual. Especially delight in the abundance of joy that comes from His presence. Satan will always offer you substitutes. Refuse them!

October 31

THE HIGHEST CALLING

*Whoever of you does not forsake
all that he has cannot be My disciple.*
LUKE 14:33

When the Standard Oil Company was looking for a representative in the Far East, they approached a missionary and offered him $10,000. He turned down the offer. They raised it to $25,000, and he turned it down again. They raised it to $50,000, and he rejected it once more.

"What's wrong?" they asked.

He replied, "Your price is all right, but your job is too small." God had called him to be a missionary, and anything else was not worthy of his consideration.

What should we be for Jesus Christ? Most Christians are not called to be missionaries or preachers, but they are called to follow Christ. They are called to be faithful wherever He puts them—in the school, in the home, in the factory or office, in the neighborhood and nation. They are called to be controlled by the Spirit and to bear the fruit of the Spirit. They are called to be Christ's ambassadors wherever God puts them.

Nothing less than God's call is worthy of our consideration.

November

*Pray that God will pour out His
Holy Spirit in Matthew homes
across North America and draw
unprecedented numbers of
people to Himself.*

November 1

PRAYER PARTNERS WITH GOD

*The Spirit Himself makes intercession for
us with groanings which cannot be uttered.*
ROMANS 8:26

Have you ever faced a situation that was so
overwhelming or so confusing you didn't even
know how to pray about it? Have you ever
been so overcome with grief or burdened by heartache
you couldn't put your emotions into words—much less
pray about them?

What a comfort these words should be: "The Spirit
helps us in our weakness. We do not know what we
ought to pray for, but the Spirit intercedes for God's
people . . . in accordance with the will of God"
(Rom. 8:26–27, NIV).

Think of it: Even when we don't know how to pray,
the Spirit knows our needs, and He brings the deepest
cries of our hearts before the throne of God. In ways
we will never understand this side of eternity, God the
Holy Spirit pleads for us before God the Father.

Turn to God in every situation—even when you
don't feel like it. The Spirit is interceding for you, in
accordance with God's will.

November 2

TRUE HAPPINESS

Happy is the man who has the
God of Jacob as his helper.
PSALM 146:5, TLB

Sometimes I almost wish Thomas Jefferson
had not inserted those words in the American
Declaration of Independence about "the pursuit
of happiness."

He was correct, of course; God has given us the
"right" (or at least the freedom) to pursue happiness.
The problem is that millions think this must be the
primary purpose of life, and they spend their lives
frantically pursuing it. In the end, however, their
search ends in disillusionment.

Happiness is a byproduct of something greater, not
an end in itself. Happiness cannot be pursued and
caught, anymore than one can pursue a sunny day,
put it in a bottle, and then bring it out on a rainy day
to enjoy again.

True happiness comes from a different pursuit—the
pursuit of God. He has promised, "You will seek Me
and find Me, when you search for Me with all your
heart" (Jer. 29:13). That promise is true—because God
also pursues us. He even sent His Son into the world
to pursue us and bring us to Heaven.

November 3

FAMILIES OF FAITH

Through wisdom a house is built,
and by understanding it is established.
PROVERBS 24:3

The family is the most important institution in the world. It was God's idea in the first place. It was not the invention of sociologists or economists or government bureaucrats who decided it would make society operate more smoothly. Families existed before cities and governments, before written language, nations, temples, and churches.

In the home, character and integrity are formed, values are made clear, and goals are set. These last a lifetime. And if they aren't formed correctly, that, too, will result in patterns—bad patterns—that last a lifetime, if God doesn't intervene.

Today, Satan is attacking the family as never before. But what are our defenses against such attacks?

As always, our best defense is the Word of God. Read the Bible together as a family. Have family devotions. Pray for one another daily by name. Be on guard against the forces that tend to pull families apart today. And most of all, commit your marriage to Christ, and make Him the center of your home—and your life.

November 4

THE UNCERTAINTY OF LIFE

*Teach us to number our days, that
we may gain a heart of wisdom.*
PSALM 90:12

We are not the masters of our fate. We think we control our lives—but we don't. In an instant life can radically change—a car accident, a heart attack, a pink slip, a child's raging fever. Frustrated researchers conquer one deadly virus, only to discover one even more lethal.

The Psalmist pointed out our basic dilemma: "Our days may come to seventy years, or eighty, if our strength endures; yet the best of them are but trouble and sorrow, for they quickly pass, and we fly away" (Ps. 90:10, NIV). Even if we live to a ripe old age, he said, we seldom know peace.

No book is more realistic about the human situation than the Bible. It won't let us get by with frothy platitudes or unsupported optimism. But it also gives us hope. It tells us Christ can change our lives, and He has prepared a perfect place for us in Heaven.

Even your next breath is a gift from God. Don't take life for granted, but "gain a heart of wisdom."

November 5

SATISFYING THE SOUL

Direct me in the path of your commands,
for there I find delight.
PSALM 119:35, NIV

The Bible teaches that a person is more than just a body—each of us is actually a living soul! Our souls are created in the image of God. God Himself has implanted His own nature within us!

Just as our bodies have certain characteristics and appetites, so do our souls. The characteristics of the soul include intelligence, emotions, and will. The human soul or spirit longs for peace, contentment, and happiness. Most of all, the soul has an appetite for God—a yearning to be reconciled to its Creator and to have fellowship with Him forever.

In our world, we give most of our attention to satisfying the appetites of the body and practically none to the soul. Consequently we are one-sided. We become fat physically and materially, while spiritually we are lean, weak, and anemic.

The soul actually demands as much attention as the body. It demands fellowship and communion with God. It demands worship, quietness, and meditation. Nothing but God ever completely satisfies, because the soul was made for God. Don't starve your soul.

November 6

THE WEAPONS OF FAITH

*This is the victory that overcomes
the world, our faith.*

1 JOHN 5:4, RSV

One of Satan's sly devices is to divert our minds from the help God offers us in our struggles against evil, telling us we have to fight the battle alone. But God knows we need His help.

The Bible warns, "Be sober, be vigilant; because your adversary the devil walks about like a roaring lion, seeking whom he may devour" (1 Pet. 5:8). What would you do if you met a lion? You'd probably run, and you'd probably grab any weapon you could to fend him off if he attacked.

And that is true in our struggles against evil. When evil and temptation stalk us, our first response should be to flee. And when they still attack, we should use every weapon we have to drive them away. The good news is this: God has provided the weapons! His Word, His angels, His Spirit, the encouragement and prayers of our brothers and sisters in Christ—these and more are "weapons" God provides.

We aren't in this battle alone—so why act like it?

November 7

What Is Joy?

The joy of the Lord is your strength.
NEHEMIAH 8:10

Some people think Christians should always be smiling and happy, and something is wrong if they aren't.

But this isn't necessarily true. Jesus stood outside the tomb of His friend Lazarus, and we read that "Jesus wept" (John 11:35). As He approached Jerusalem "He saw the city and wept" (Luke 19:41) because of its spiritual blindness and guilt. He knelt in the Garden of Gethsemane and was "in agony ... [and] His sweat became like great drops of blood" (Luke 22:44).

Don't confuse happiness with joy. Happiness comes with happy circumstances; joy wells up deep inside our souls as we learn to trust Christ. Joy does not mean that we are never sad or that we never cry. But joy is a quiet confidence, a state of inner peace that comes from God.

Life's troubles will rob us of our happiness, but they can never rob us of the joy God gives us, as we turn in faith to Him and seek His face.

November 8

BOUNDLESS BLESSINGS

He gathers the lambs in his arms
and carries them close to his heart.

ISAIAH 40:11, NIV

The Old Testament gives a wonderful picture of God as our Shepherd. One Psalm begins, "Hear us, Shepherd of Israel, you who lead Joseph like a flock" (Ps. 80:1, NIV). The almighty Creator of the universe stoops to be the Shepherd of His people!

A shepherd protects and feeds his sheep, and pursues them when they stray. At evening he brings them into the fold, secure against every enemy. Without the shepherd, the sheep would scatter and wander into danger.

In the best-known of all Psalms, David makes the relationship personal. "The Lord is my shepherd," he cries exultantly, "I lack nothing" (Ps. 23:1, NIV). He then tells of God's constant care, until that day when "I will dwell in the house of the LORD forever" (Ps. 23:6, NIV).

But the New Testament tells of another Shepherd— the Lord Jesus Christ: "I am the good shepherd. The good shepherd gives His life for the sheep" (John 10:11). He guides and protects us, and even gave His life so we will be safely in His fold forever.

November 9

BANISHING WORRY

The Lord is near to all who call upon Him,
to all who call upon Him in truth.
PSALM 145:18

Think of the things you do *not* worry about. Perhaps you never worry about whether you will be able to get water out of the faucet in your kitchen, or maybe you do not worry about a tree falling on your house. You may be a worrier by nature, but even the worst worrier in the world doesn't worry about *some* things!

Now ask yourself why you do not worry about such things. Is it because, in the case of running water, it has always been there when you wanted it? Or that a tree has never fallen on your house before? Certainty breeds trust, doesn't it? (You may even live in a place where there are no tall trees.)

We can be just as certain and just as worry-free about God's love and protection. What is the evidence? It is the Cross, where God fully expressed His love for us. The Bible says, "He who did not spare his own Son, but gave him up for us all—how will he not also, along with him, graciously give us all things?" (Rom. 8:32, NIV). His love is certain. He has never gone back on a single promise, and He never will.

CREATED IN HIS IMAGE

If anyone is in Christ, he is a new creation.
2 CORINTHIANS 5:17

Is it not logical to believe that the only One who can re-create us is the One who created us in the first place? If your watch were out of order, you wouldn't take it to a blacksmith. If your car needed overhauling, you wouldn't take it to a plumber. If you needed an operation, you wouldn't go to a machine shop.

Our spiritual problems can only be solved by the God who created us originally. He created us in His own image and likeness, and He knows all about us.

Today by the grace of His Son, He can re-create us in the likeness of His resurrection. Through faith in Jesus Christ, we are recreated and become partakers of His life. Just as we were born again by the Spirit of God, so we grow and become more like Christ as the Spirit works in our lives.

"Therefore, if anyone is in Christ, he is a new creation; old things have passed away; behold, all things have become new" (2 Cor. 5:17). Don't be chained to the past. You are a new creation in Christ!

November 11

A Home in Heaven

You yourselves had [in heaven]
a better and lasting possession.
Hebrews 10:34, ab

Paul once wrote, "If only for this life we have hope in Christ, we are of all people most to be pitied" (1 Cor. 15:19, NIV). If there is no life after death, no Heaven, no promise of a better world—then life is empty, hopeless, without meaning or purpose.

But this life is not all! Ahead is Heaven, and someday "we shall always be with the Lord" (1 Thess. 4:17). Someday we will go to a home where all is happiness, joy, and peace. How barren our lives would be if we didn't have this hope.

Knowing Heaven is real will make a difference in the way we live. For one thing, we won't become attached to the things of this world. We will say with Paul, "I have learned in whatever state I am, to be content" (Phil. 4:11).

But Heaven should also give us a burden for those who do not have this hope. Every day you meet people who do not know Christ. Will you tell them?

November 12

A United Family

All your children shall be taught by the Lord,
and great shall be the peace of your children.

ISAIAH 54:13

The family is the basic unit of society. But from the very beginning, since man sinned against God, the family has been in trouble. The first crime we read about in the Bible occurred when Cain killed his brother Abel. Instead of love, family life all too often became marked by conflict and tension.

For best results in marriage and building a stable home, follow the instructions of the One who performed the first wedding in the Garden of Eden. Those instructions are in the Bible. The reason the family is in critical condition today is that we have neglected His rules for a successful home. We have put self in place of sacrifice. We have valued things more than we have valued people.

You can have the right kind of home. Your home can be united if it is now divided. The place to begin is on your knees, asking Christ for forgiveness and then asking God to give you a new love for each other—and for Him. Don't let your family drift apart, but with God's help resist the pressures and come together around the Cross.

November 13

CLING AND HOPE

The Lord will be a shelter for His people.
JOEL 3:16

The late British historian, Arnold Toynbee, gave his personal slogan to the world when he said, "Cling, and hope." In other words, he says, all the ideals we held a few years ago are crumbling; but he advised the human race to cling and hope.

But to what? Millions cling to the wreckage they have made of their lives, thinking they have nowhere else to turn. Others cling to false ideologies or deceptive cults. Still others cling to possessions, or relationships, or pleasures. Yes, "cling, and hope"—but what if you are clinging to something that is sinking?

However, thousands still find refuge from the storms of life by their living faith in a living God!

To turn to God in an hour such as this in the history of the world is not escapism. Multiplied thousands have found that faith in Christ is more than adequate for the pressures of this hour.

The true Christian does more than "cling and hope." He knows that with Christ he is secure forever. Is your hope in Him?

November 14

GOD IN HUMAN FORM

*[Christ] has gone into heaven and
is at the right hand of God.*

1 PETER 3:22

What proofs did Jesus offer that He was truly God come in human form?

First, there was the proof of His perfect life. He could ask, "Which of you convicts me of sin?" (John 8:46)—and no one could answer.

Second, there was the evidence of His miraculous power. His power was the power of God Almighty.

Third, there was the evidence of fulfilled prophecy. Hundreds of years before His birth the prophets of the Old Testament spoke precisely of His death, and resurrection.

Fourth, there was the evidence of His resurrection from the dead.

Fifth, there is the proof of changed lives. Christ alone, the divine Son of God, has power to change the human heart. And He does.

Faith in Christ is not a "leap in the dark." It is based on the solid facts of Christ's life, death, and resurrection. Thank God we have a solid foundation in Him!

November 15

"Even So, Come!"

Behold, I am coming quickly.
Revelation 22:7

What would you say about a person who had made a hundred promises to you and already kept ninety-nine of them? You probably would think he was honest enough to fulfill the last promise as well, wouldn't you?

Jesus Christ has fulfilled every promise He ever made, except one. He has not yet returned. Will He?

In both the Old and New Testaments there are references to the return of the Lord. Isaiah, for example, looked forward to the day when the Messiah's kingdom would be a reality: "Behold, I create new heavens and a new earth; and the former shall not be remembered or come to mind" (Is. 65:17).

John quotes Christ as saying "I go to prepare a place for you. And . . . I will come again and receive you to Myself" (John 14:2–3). The entire book of Revelation tells of the glorious return of Christ. And we can say with the apostle John, who wrote that book, "Amen. Even so, come, Lord Jesus" (Rev. 22:20).

Are you looking forward to His return? And are you seeking until that day to be His faithful servant?

November 16

DEALING WITH ETERNITY

*I will see Your face in righteousness; I shall be
satisfied when I awake in your likeness.*

PSALM 17:15

When English patriot Sir William Russell
went to the scaffold in 1683, he took his
watch out of his pocket and handed it to the
physician who attended him in his death. "Would you
kindly take my timepiece?" he asked. "I have no use
for it. I am now dealing with eternity."

This world fades into insignificance in the light of
eternity. All the things that preoccupy us are no longer
important, and only one thing counts: our relationship
with God.

But we should live every day in light of eternity! As
Peter wrote in his last letter, "Since all these things will
be dissolved, what manner of persons ought you to be
in holy conduct and godliness? . . . Be diligent to be
found by Him in peace, without spot and blameless"
(2 Pet. 3:11, 14).

How different would today be if you knew it would
be your last one on earth before meeting God face to
face? We should strive to live every day as if it were
our last, for one day it will be!

November 17

WE WILL SEE HIM

Our days on earth are as a shadow.
1 CHRONICLES 29:15

C. S. Lewis once observed that this life is only "shadow lands" compared with the glory to come. Even life at its best is but a shadow of Heaven.

Does that mean we turn our backs on this world and have nothing to do with its delights? Not necessarily. Sometimes (as Lewis was suggesting) the good things God gives us are a foreshadowing, a hint of what is to come. We experience the joy of marriage, knowing it is the foretaste of an even greater joy: the heavenly marriage feast of the Lamb (Rev. 19:9). We enjoy the beauty of God's creation, knowing it is the foretaste of an even greater beauty; the glory of Heaven (Rev. 21:23).

Take delight in the good things God gives you. Don't be too preoccupied to "smell the roses"! The Bible reminds us, "Every good gift and every perfect gift is from above, and comes down from the Father of lights" (James 1:17). And every one of His good gifts should remind us of the glory to come!

November 18

SWEET SLUMBER

I will ... lie down in peace ... for you
alone ... make me dwell in safety.
PSALM 4:8

By any measure drug and alcohol dependence has become one of our greatest social problems. The issue isn't just illegal drugs; many depend on alcohol or over-the-counter or prescription drugs just to face each day or to get to sleep at night.

I'm not a doctor, of course, and I fully realize some drugs have a legitimate place under careful medical supervision. But in my experience far too many people turn first to drugs or alcohol instead of to God. Rather than face their problems and deal with them (with God's help), they use drugs or alcohol to escape.

But such "solutions" never work, and in fact only make things worse. No wonder the book of Proverbs warns that alcohol "at the last ... bites like a serpent, and stings like a viper" (Prov. 23:32).

Don't let anything substitute for God. He loves you, and He wants to give you peace—the peace that comes from knowing Him. Jesus' promise to His followers is true: "I will give you rest" (Matt. 11:28).

November 19

SUNSHINE AND SHADOW

*If you should suffer for righteousness'
sake, you are blessed.*
1 PETER 3:14

All the masterpieces of painting contain both light and shadow. By them the artist highlights certain features of his subject, and they provide contrast and harmony to reveal beauty or character.

A happy life is not one filled only with sunshine, but one that uses both light and shadow to produce beauty. Suffering or persecution can become a blessing because they can form a dark backdrop for the radiance of the Christian life. The greatest musicians as a rule are those who know how to bring song out of sadness. Fanny Crosby, her spirit aglow with faith in Christ, saw more with her sightless eyes than most of us do with normal vision. She gave us some of the great gospel songs that cheer our hearts and lives.

Paul and Silas sang a song of praise at midnight in a rat-infested jail in Philippi, their feet in stocks, their backs raw from the jailer's whip. But their patience in suffering and persecution led to the conversion of the heathen prison warden and his family.

Don't despise the shadows God brings into your life. He can use them to produce a masterpiece.

November 20

ABIDING PEACE

Fear not, for I am with you; be not
dismayed, for I am your God.
ISAIAH 41:10

Whenever I think of God's faithfulness in the midst of suffering I am reminded of my dear late friend Corrie ten Boom, the remarkable Dutch woman who (with her family) hid Jews from the Nazis. After being imprisoned in Ravensbrück, the infamous concentration camp, Corrie traveled the world telling her story of suffering, forgiveness, and joy.

For thirty-five years she never had a permanent home, but when she was eighty-five and in declining health, some friends provided her with a lovely house in California. It was a luxury she never dreamed she would have (and one she never would have pursued on her own).

One day her friend, the late movie director James Collier, was visiting. He said, "Corrie, hasn't God been good to give you this beautiful house?" She replied firmly, "Jimmy, God was good when I was in Ravensbrück, too!"

Most of us will never experience the horrors Corrie knew. But no matter what we face, we can depend on God's promise: "Fear not; for I am with you."

November 21

THANKFUL IN PRAYER

Devote yourselves to prayer, being watchful and thankful.
COLOSSIANS 4:2, NIV

Prayer isn't just asking God for something we want. Prayer should also include confession of sin, and praise to God for who He is and what He has done for us.

But prayer should have an additional element, and that is thanksgiving. Repeatedly the Bible commands us to give thanks. The Psalmist said, "Oh, give thanks to the LORD, for He is good! For His mercy endures forever"(Ps. 107:1). Jesus only distributed the bread He had miraculously provided for the crowds after "he had given thanks" (Matt. 15:36, NIV). At the Last Supper with His disciples, before facing the horror of the Cross, Jesus "gave thanks" (Luke 22:17, 19).

It's easy to be thankful when God blesses us with something good—swift recovery from an illness, for example, or an advancement at work. But the Bible says we should "give thanks in *all* circumstances, for this is God's will for [us] in Christ Jesus" (1 Thess. 5:18, NIV, italics mine).

Thankfulness drives away a sour or prideful spirit. Make it part of your prayers every day.

November 22

THE GRACE OF GRATITUDE

It is good to give thanks to the Lord.
PSALM 92:1

The Pilgrim Fathers who landed at Plymouth in America in 1620 knew nothing of the bountiful prosperity that so many people enjoy today. During that first long winter, seven times as many graves were made for the dead as homes were built for the living. Seed, imported from England, failed to grow, and a ship that was to bring food and relief, brought thirty-five more mouths to feed, but not an ounce of provisions. They caught fish, hunted wild fowl, and venison. They had a little English meal and some Indian corn.

Yet their lives were marked by a spirit of constant thankfulness. On one occasion William Brewster, rising from a scanty Plymouth dinner of clams and water, gave thanks to God "for the abundance of the sea and the treasures hid in the sand."

According to today's standards, they had little; but they possessed a sense of great gratitude. Gratitude is one of the greatest Christian graces; ingratitude, one of the most vicious sins. Ask God to open your eyes to all the blessings He has bestowed on you, and to give you a fresh spirit of gratitude—not just at this season of the year, but always.

November 23

GOD'S HOLINESS

Holy, holy, holy is the Lord of hosts;
the whole earth is full of His glory!
ISAIAH 6:3

The Bible teaches that God is absolutely holy and pure. From Genesis to Revelation, God reveals Himself as so holy He cannot even look on sin.

Christ cried from the Cross, "My God, My God, why have You forsaken Me?" (Mark 15:34). What a horrible moment, as the blackness of human sin—now laid upon Christ—caused the Father to turn away in disgust. In that moment Jesus endured the ultimate punishment for our sins—the punishment of being banished from the presence of His Father on our behalf.

If you were asked to list the things you are thankful for, what would you include? Perhaps your family, health, friends, church—and those wouldn't be wrong. We should be grateful for every gift God gives us.

But the greatest gift of all is the gift of His Son, who endured the penalty we deserved for our sin, so we could be reconciled to a holy God. Never take that gift for granted! "Thanks be to God for his indescribable gift!" (2 Cor. 9:15).

November 24

TRUE THANKSGIVING

Oh, give thanks to the Lord, for He is good!
PSALM 107:1

Separated from friends, unjustly accused, brutally treated—if any man had a right to complain it was this man, languishing almost forgotten in a harsh Roman prison. But instead of complaints, his lips rang with words of praise and thanksgiving!

This was the apostle Paul—a man who had learned the meaning of true thanksgiving, even in the midst of great adversity. Look carefully at what he wrote during that prison experience: "Sing and make music from your heart to the Lord, always giving thanks to God the Father for everything, in the name of our Lord Jesus Christ" (Eph. 5:19–20, NIV).

Think of it! "Always giving thanks . . . for everything" no matter the circumstances. His guards and fellow prisoners must have thought him crazy—but that didn't stop him. Thanksgiving for Paul was not a once-a-year celebration, but a daily reality that made him a joyful person in every situation. May that be true of us.

November 25

GOD'S LOVE

In this the love of God was made manifest...,
that God sent his only Son into the world.
1 JOHN 4:9, RSV

From Genesis to Revelation, from earth's greatest tragedy to earth's greatest triumph, the dramatic story of humanity's lowest depths and God's highest heights can be couched in twenty-five beautiful words: "For God so loved the world that He gave His only begotten Son, that whoever believes in Him should not perish but have everlasting life" (John 3:16).

Many people misunderstand God's attribute of love. "God is love" does not mean that everything is sweet, beautiful, and happy, and that God's love could not possibly allow punishment for sin.

God's holiness demands that all sin be punished, but God's love provided a plan of redemption and salvation for a lost and sinful world. By that plan Jesus Christ came from Heaven to give His life as the final and perfect sacrifice for sin.

But we must respond. We must believe. We must commit our lives to Jesus Christ and trust Him as our Savior and Lord. Have you put your faith in Him? If so, everlasting life is yours!

November 26

WISDOM FROM ABOVE

The wisdom that is from above is first pure, then peaceable.
JAMES 3:17

Today there is more knowledge in the world than ever before. Computers or fiber optic cables can transmit information in a millisecond to any part of the globe. More facts have been discovered in the past century than in all of the other centuries of human history combined. Yet that same century also recorded the most devastating wars and the fiercest genocides in human history. We have never been farther from solving our basic problems.

The Bible says there are two kinds of wisdom in the world. First, there is wisdom that is given by God, a wisdom that views life in terms of eternity. Of this wisdom, the Scripture says, "The wisdom that is from above is first pure, then peaceable, gentle, willing to yield, full of mercy and good fruits, without partiality and without hypocrisy" (James 3:17).

The second is the "wisdom of the world." This wisdom excludes God and His moral standards from human decisions, and seeks to solve society's problems apart from Him. But where has it gotten us? Which kind of wisdom will you choose?

November 27

TRAVELING TO HEAVEN

The Lord will ... preserve me for His heavenly kingdom.
2 TIMOTHY 4:18

Preparing for Heaven is much like going on a journey. First, you must decide you want to go there. Next, you must purchase your ticket.

But wait! How will you purchase it? Can you buy it by being a good person? Or going to church or acting religious? Or giving money or volunteering your time to help others? The Bible says none of these will suffice, because the ticket to Heaven is expensive—far too expensive for any human being to afford.

Does that mean we can never go there? No—and the reason is because Someone else has already purchased the ticket for us. That person was Jesus Christ, and the price He paid was His own blood, shed on the Cross for us.

Now He offers us the ticket to Heaven free and fully paid! Why refuse it? Why try some other way? Jesus' invitation is still open: "Come! Let the one who is thirsty come; and let the one who wishes take the free gift of the water of life" (Rev. 22:17, NIV).

Giving to God

Honor the Lord with your possessions, and
with the firstfruits of all your increase.

God doesn't "need" our money to get His work done. He is sovereign and could do it without our help. Yet He has arranged it so that His work often depends on our generosity.

At least two things happen when we give. First, when we give with the right attitude, God reminds us that what we have isn't really ours. He gave us everything we have, and it actually belongs to Him. King David prayed, "All things come from You, and of Your own we have given You" (1 Chron. 29:14). We need to learn that truth.

Second, when we give, we help meet the needs of others whom God also loves. By giving to others we testify to God's love for them, and we point them to the greatest gift of all—God's gift of His Son for our salvation.

Someone has said that our lives should resemble channels, not reservoirs. A reservoir stores water; a channel distributes it. God wants us to be channels of blessing to others. Are you?

November 29

A HEAVENLY ADDRESS

I am going there to prepare a place for you.
JOHN 14:2, NIV

I live in a place, high on a mountain in a log cabin in North Carolina. I may travel all over the world, but I know that when I come home, I will return to a precise location. It will still be there at the end of my journey, and I always look forward to coming home!

In saying that He was going to prepare a place for us, Jesus was telling us that when we die, we are going to a precise location. We do not evaporate or disappear. In fact, He said, "In my Father's house are many mansions" (John 14:2). We are going to have a place in Heaven if we have trusted Christ as our Savior—and not only a place, but a mansion!

When we as Christians die, we go straight into the presence of Christ—straight to that place, straight to that mansion in Heaven to spend eternity with God. We are simply changing our address!

November 30

GOD'S TRUTH

You are my hiding place . . . ; I hope in Your word.
PSALM 119:114

God's Word never changes. Jesus said, "For truly I tell you, until heaven and earth disappear, not the smallest letter, not the least stroke of a pen, will by any means disappear from the Law" (Matt. 5:18, NIV). He also declared, "Heaven and earth will pass away, but My words will by no means pass away" (Matt. 24:35).

This isn't because God is an inflexible or insensitive tyrant. It is because He knows what is best for us. He knows how we function, and He knows the pitfalls and dangers we face. If He didn't love us, He wouldn't try to guide us in the right path. But He does!

Only God's Word can help us avoid moral and spiritual danger, and lead us in the right way. The Psalmist testified, "Your word is a lamp to my feet and a light to my path. . . . The entrance of Your words gives light" (Ps. 119:105, 130).

Let God's Word shape and guide you. God loves you too much to leave you in the dark!

December

Pray for those who received Jesus Christ during My Hope with Billy Graham, *that they would grow in their faith and become active members of a local Christian fellowship.*

December 1

INFINITE GRACE

Grace and truth came through Jesus Christ.
JOHN 1:17

The word *grace* means more than just God's kindness or gentleness toward us, or even His mercy. It means His undeserved favor. It means God owes nothing to us, and we deserve nothing from Him. When the Bible says "by grace you have been saved" (Eph. 2:5), it means our salvation was totally unmerited. It came solely because of God's grace.

The *motive* of grace is the infinite, compassionate love of a merciful God, but the *work* of grace was Christ's death on the Cross. When I imagine Christ hanging from the Cross, the spikes in His hands, the crown of thorns on His brow, His blood draining from His body, the soldiers mocking Him—then I begin to see the depth of God's grace. Then I know that nothing can equal the infinite love of God for a sinful world.

But God's grace is also exhibited when we humbly bow before Christ in repentance and faith, for then we find forgiveness. Thank God for His grace, for without it we would have no hope!

December 2

SIN'S DEADLY HERITAGE

The creation itself will be liberated from its bondage to decay.

ROMANS 8:21, NIV

Recently some computers in our office were attacked by a major computer virus. Thinking they were opening a legitimate e-mail, the staff suddenly found their computers running amuck, unable to function as they were designed to do. Only a major reprogramming of their corrupted hard drives, I was told, restored them to usefulness.

I couldn't help but compare this to another virus—the "virus" of sin. God created our first parents perfect and without sin, their every need met and their relationship with God unblemished. But then they rebelled against God, sin entered the world—and since that day, the human heart has been infected with the deadly "virus" of sin. Our fellowship with God was destroyed, we became morally weak and corrupt, and even all creation was affected.

But Christ came to conquer the "virus" of sin! When He enters our lives, He begins to remake us from within. The "virus" no longer has absolute control. And someday God will remove the "virus" of sin forever, and all creation will be renewed.

December 3

FROM TIME TO ETERNITY

We give thanks to God . . . because of the
hope which is laid up for you in heaven.
COLOSSIAN 1:3, 5

Once I stood in London to watch Queen
Elizabeth return from an overseas trip. I saw the
parade of dignitaries, the marching bands, the
crack troops, the waving flags. I saw all the splendor
that accompanies the homecoming of a queen.

However, that was nothing compared to the
homecoming of a true believer. At that moment of
death, the believer enters Heaven itself, carried upward
by the angels to the glorious welcome awaiting the
redeemed (Luke 16:22).

From our human viewpoint death is always tinged
with sadness. It is not wrong to mourn the loss of a
loved one; Jesus wept at the grave of His friend Lazarus
(John 11:35).

But the Christian should never consider the death of
a fellow believer as a tragedy. Paul said we should not
"grieve like the rest of mankind, who have no hope"
(1 Thess. 4:13, NIV). Yes, we have hope! The way to
Heaven may lie through the valley of the shadow of
death, but the angels accompany us all the way—and
beyond is Heaven, our glorious home.

December 4

PEACE IN PAIN

So walk in Him rooted and built up in Him.
COLOSSIANS 2:6–7

Not far from our home in North Carolina is Mt. Mitchell, the highest point in the eastern United States. On its ridges are old trees that have been stunted and gnarled by the hostile climate and the sparse rocky soil.

But local craftsmen have told me that if one of these trees finally dies, its wood is highly prized—and the reason is because it is so strong. The tree resisted those fierce alpine winds for decades, and they strengthened it.

What happens when the winds of adversity blow in your life? Do they flatten you, knock you down, stop your growth? Or, like those trees, do you grow stronger?

What makes the difference? The trees that survive, I am told, are those with the deepest roots. The roots are like an anchor helping them survive the storms, and they also draw up the soil's nutrients, helping them grow stronger.

Make sure your soul is firmly planted in Christ, so you may be "rooted and built up in Him and established in the faith" (Col. 2:7).

December 5

Twice Born

Unless one is born again, he cannot
see the kingdom of God.
John 3:3

We cannot fully explain the mystery of physical birth, but we accept its wonder, and we accept the fact of new life. What is it, then, that keeps us from accepting the reality and wonder of spiritual rebirth—of being "born again"? To those who have experienced it or seen it happen in others, it is just as real as physical birth.

Just as surely as God implants the life cell in the tiny seed that produces the mighty oak . . . as surely as He instills the heartbeat in the life of the tiny infant yet unborn . . . as surely as He puts motion into the planets, stars, and heavenly bodies—so He implants His divine life in the hearts of those who earnestly seek Him through Christ.

This is not conjecture; it is fact. But has it happened to you? If not, you are not only unfit for the Kingdom of God—you are cheating yourself out of the greatest, most revolutionary experience known to any human being. By a simple prayer of faith ask Christ into your life right now. He will come in, and you will be born again!

December 6

THE JOY OF CHRISTMAS

When they saw the star, they rejoiced
with exceedingly great joy.
MATTHEW 2:10

Every year people write me saying how much they dread Christmas. Often their complaint stems from how busy they will be, or how much money they will spend.

Did those wise men who journeyed hundreds of miles across the desert to seek out the infant Jesus ever feel that way? After all, it took months to make the arduous trip, and they had gone to great expense to provide gifts of gold, frankincense, and myrrh for the new child.

I doubt it. In fact, as their journey neared its end we read they had "exceedingly great joy." What made the difference? Their focus was totally on Jesus, the One who would be called "Immanuel, . . . God with us" (Matt. 1:23).

Don't let this Christmas season overwhelm you. Don't feel you have to do everything, or go into debt just to impress other people. Focus instead on Jesus. Take time every day to read the prophecies of His coming, and the wonderful story of His birth. Make this Christmas one of "exceedingly great joy"!

December 7

GOD SEES ALL

Great is our Lord, and mighty in power;
His understanding is infinite.
PSALM 147:5

Some years ago a friend of mine was standing on top of a mountain in North Carolina. The roads in those days were filled with curves, and it was difficult to see very far ahead. This man saw two cars heading toward each other. He realized they couldn't see each other. A third car pulled up and began to pass one of the cars, although there wasn't enough space to see the other car approaching around the bend. My friend shouted a warning, but the drivers couldn't hear, and there was a fatal crash.

This is how God looks upon us in His omniscience. He sees what has happened, what is happening, and what will happen. He also sees us when we foolishly think we can get by with breaking His moral laws, or we act out of sinful pride or lust or anger. Like the man on that mountain, He shouts His warnings at us—but we are too busy or too stubborn to listen.

God sees the whole picture. He knows what is best for us, and He knows what will destroy us. Don't think your way is better than His, but listen to His Word—and obey.

Training Our Children

*Train up a child in the way he should go, and
when he is old he will not depart from it.*

PROVERBS 22:6

C hildren need to know right and wrong, and the
best place to learn it is at home. If they don't
learn it there, they may end up without any
moral and spiritual anchor.

Children also want their parents to care enough for
them to be strict. Parents who refuse to discipline their
children are actually sending a signal, saying they
don't care what happens to them. The Bible says, "He
who loves him disciplines him promptly" (Prov. 13:24).

The Bible also says to train our children in God's
ways "precept upon precept, line upon line . . . here
a little, there a little" (Is. 28:10). In other words, when
a child is about to become a teenager, we can't
suddenly say, "I've ignored it so far, but now I'll cram
religion and morals into my child." It must start the
very moment he or she has any understanding.

But what we do is as important as what we
say, for children usually acquire their parents'
characteristics and habits. What are our children (and
grandchildren) learning from us?

December 9

PERIL OF PREOCCUPATION

Behold, God is great, and we do not know Him.
JOB 36:26

One evening in Jerusalem I looked out my hotel window and saw the lights of Bethlehem in the distance. I thought about the response of the innkeeper when Mary and Joseph wanted to find a room where the Child could be born. The innkeeper was not hostile; he was not opposed to them but his inn was crowded, his hands were full, and his mind was preoccupied.

Perhaps he told them, "I wish I could help you, but I must keep my priorities. After all, this is a business, and this coming Child is no real concern of mine. But I'm not a hardhearted man. Over there is the stable. You are welcome to use it if you care to. That is the best I can do. Now I must get back to my work. My guests need me."

And this is the answer that millions give today. It is the answer of preoccupation—not fierce opposition, not furious hatred, but unconcern about spiritual things. We are simply too preoccupied with other things to welcome Christ into our lives. Don't let that happen to you!

OUR JOURNEY TO GOD

*He is able to keep what I have
committed to Him until that Day.*

2 TIMOTHY 1:12

The Bible speaks of death as a departure. When Paul approached the valley of the shadow of death he did not shudder with fear; rather he announced with a note of triumph, "The time of my departure is at hand" (2 Tim. 4:6).

The word *departure* in Paul's time literally meant to pull up anchor and set sail. Everything that happens prior to death is a preparation for the journey. Just as a ship would be loaded with provisions and the voyage carefully mapped before its departure, so our time on this earth should be spent carefully preparing for our journey into eternity.

Many times I have said farewell to my wife and children as I have departed for a distant destination. Separation always brings a tinge of sadness, but there is the high hope that we shall meet again.

Such is the hope of every believing Christian as we stand at the grave of a loved one who has departed to be with the Lord. We say "Goodbye," but only until that new day dawns and we are together with the Lord.

December 11

GOD SENT HIS SON

In Him dwells all the fullness of the Godhead bodily.
COLOSSIANS 2:9

On that first Christmas night in Bethlehem, "God was manifested in the flesh" (1 Tim. 3:16). This manifestation was in the person of Jesus Christ.

What an incredible truth! Think of it: The God of the universe came down from Heaven that first Christmas night and took human form! As the words of the familiar Christmas carol declare, "Veiled in flesh the Godhead see; hail th' incarnate Deity."

If you want to know what God is like, then take a long look at Jesus Christ—because He was God in human flesh. In Him were displayed not only the perfections that had been exhibited in the creation— such as wisdom, power, and majesty—but also such perfections as justice, mercy, grace, and love. "The Word was God.... And the Word became flesh and dwelt among us" (John 1:1, 14).

To His disciples Jesus said, "You believe in God, believe also in Me" (John 14:1). This sequence of faith is inevitable. If we believe in what God made and what God said, we will believe in the One whom God sent.

December 12

THE ANTHEM OF HIS NAME

God also has . . . given Him the
name which is above every name.
PHILIPPIANS 2:9

O ver two thousand years ago, on a night the world has come to call Christmas, a young Jewish maiden went through the experience countless mothers had before her: She brought forth a child.

But this birth was like no other in the history of the human race. For one thing, this Child had no human father. As the angel had promised, "The Holy Spirit will come upon you, and the power of the Highest will overshadow you" (Luke 1:35). In humble obedience the Virgin Mary responded, "Let it be to me according to your word" (Luke 1:38).

But it also was like no other birth because of the One who was born. This was no ordinary child. This was the unique Son of God, sent from Heaven to save us from our sins.

Amid the glitter and busyness of the season, don't lose sight of the miracle of that first Christmas. With the wise men, let us fall down and worship Him (Matt. 2:11).

December 13

THE NIGHT OF LIGHT

I am the light of the world.
He who follows Me shall not walk in darkness.
JOHN 8:12

This month the birthday of Jesus Christ will be celebrated all over the world. It will be celebrated in various ways, in many languages, by people of all races. For a few hours many in the world will stop talking of satellites, rockets, and war. For a few hours they will talk of peace on earth and good will toward men. People will exchange their gifts and talk about the Prince of Peace.

Imagine the scene in Bethlehem two thousand years ago. It was the night of nights, and yet it had begun as every other night had before it.

But it was to become the greatest, most significant night of history. This was the night that would conquer darkness and bring in the day when there would be no more night. This was the night when those who sat in darkness would see a great light. This was the night God brought into the world the One who is "the light of the world."

May His light shine in your life this Christmas season!

Our Loving, Compassionate God

I am the bread of life.
John 6:35

Jesus came to the world so we could know, once and for all, that God is concerned about the way we live, the way we believe, and the way we die. God could have told us in other ways, of course— and He had, throughout the pages of the Old Testament and in the lives of His people. By His written Word He declared His love.

But Jesus was the Living Word. By His life, death, and resurrection, Jesus *demonstrated* God's love in a way we could never deny. Paul wrote, "But God demonstrates His own love toward us, in that while we were still sinners, Christ died for us" (Rom. 5:8).

Every time He fed the hungry, He was saying, "I am the bread of life." Every time He healed a suffering person, He was saying, "It hurts Me to see you in pain." Every move He made, every miracle He performed, every word He spoke was for the purpose of reconciling a lost world to the loving, compassionate God.

December 15

The True Light

You are the Christ, the Son of the living God.
MATTHEW 16:16

Christ came into this world as God's Ambassador, sent from Heaven to tell us of God's love, and to bring the war between us and God to an end.

Now we, as "ambassadors for Christ" (2 Cor. 5:20), boldly echo the ringing conviction of the apostle Peter when he confessed, "You are the Christ, the Son of the living God." The title "Christ" means "anointed one." It is the term, in the Greek language, for the ancient Hebrew word "Messiah"—the anointed one whom God would send to save His people.

Peter and his fellow Jews, the first believers of the early Christian Church, recognized Jesus Christ as the Messiah promised in the Old Testament. Their world was one of discouragement and despair, but the promised Messiah shone as a beacon in the darkness, and His light has never dimmed. "In Him was life, and the life was the light of men" (John 1:4).

No matter how dark the world gets . . . no matter how dark our paths may seem . . . Jesus is still our life and light.

December 16

THE SUMMIT OF LOVE

See what great love the Father has lavished on us,
that we should be called children of God!
1 JOHN 3:1, NIV

Mary and Joseph deeply loved the Child God gave them, even becoming refugees to spare His life when King Herod tried to kill Him (Matt. 2:13).

But their love was almost nothing compared with the infinite love of God for His Son. The Bible declares, "The Father loves the Son, and has given all things into His hand" (John 3:35). Can you even begin to imagine the Father's emotions that first Christmas as His dearly loved Son left Heaven for earth, knowing He would one day go to the Cross, "despised and rejected by men, a Man of sorrows and acquainted with grief" (Isa. 53:3)?

We rightly focus on God's love for us. But don't lose sight of what it cost the Father to send His beloved Son into the world. Why did He do it? Because "God so loved the world that He gave His only begotten Son, that whoever believes in Him should not perish but have everlasting life" (John 3:16).

God loves the Son—and He loves you as well.

December 17

THE REMEDY FOR SIN

*Bless the Lord, . . . who forgives all your
iniquities, who heals all your diseases.*
PSALM 103:2–3

Jesus came into the world to save all kinds of
people: rich or poor, black or white, educated or
illiterate, sophisticated or ordinary—or anyone
in between.

Only two groups of people gathered at God's
invitation to pay Him homage when He was born.
One was the shepherds—lowly, at the bottom of the
social ladder, uneducated, unsophisticated. The other
was the wise men—intellectuals, from another race
and country, wealthy, respected. The two groups could
hardly have been more different!

God brought both groups to Bethlehem—one by an
angelic announcement, one by the appearance of a
miraculous star. And by bringing both, God was telling
us that Jesus is the Savior for everyone. Every person
stands in need of His forgiveness and new life—and
every person can know it, if he or she only repents and
makes that journey to the Christ of Christmas.

No matter who you are in the eyes of others, you
need Christ. And no matter what you have done, He
loves you and stands ready to welcome you.

December 18

PERFECT PEACE

Your faith has saved you. Go in peace.
LUKE 7:50

During the First World War, on Christmas Eve, the battlefield was strangely quiet. As the soft snow fell, the thoughts of the young men were of home and their families.

Softly one lad began to hum "Silent Night." Others took up the chorus until the trenches resounded with the Christmas song. When they finished they were astonished to hear the song echoing from the trenches across no-man's-land: In their own tongue the other soldiers also sang "Silent Night." That night they were thinking of the Prince of Peace, the Christ of Christmas.

How different this world would be if we could unite together around that "Holy Infant so tender and mild." Earth can be as Heaven with Christ. Discord can be as peace when Christ is near. Midnight gloom can be transformed into noonday brightness when He abides with us.

Full peace will come only when Christ returns. But until that day we can know His peace in our hearts and can be messengers of His peace in the world, as we commit our lives to Him.

December 19

A Rainbow of Hope

The Lord is near to all who call upon Him, . . .
who call upon Him in truth.
PSALM 145:18

Have you ever thought about what has happened because Christ has come to the world? That Babe in the manger of Bethlehem grew up to become our crucified and risen Savior—and the world has never been the same.

His compassion has made the world more compassionate. His healing touch has made the world more humanitarian. His selflessness has made the world more self-effacing. Christ drew a rainbow of hope around the shoulders of men and women and gave them something to live for.

If Christ had not come, this world would indeed be a hopeless world. If Christ had not come, this would be a lost world. There would be no access to God, there would be no atonement for sin, there would be no forgiveness, and there would be no Savior.

Yes, Christ came into the world and made it a better place. And He will do the same for you, if you will open your life to Him.

December 20

THE KING OF KINGS

A scepter of righteousness is the
scepter of Your kingdom.
PSALM 45:6

From his very birth Christ was recognized as King. Something about him inspired allegiance, loyalty, and homage. Wise men brought Him gifts. Shepherds fell down and worshiped Him. Herod, realizing that there is never room for two thrones in one kingdom, sought His life.

As Jesus began His ministry, His claims upon people's lives were total and absolute. He allowed no divided loyalty. He demanded and received complete adoration and devotion. Mature men and women left their businesses and gave themselves in complete obedience to Him. Many of them gave their lives, pouring out the last full measure of devotion.

His words caused even His most avowed enemies to say, "No man ever spoke like this Man!" (John 7:46). And yet He was more than a poet, more than a statesman, more than a physician. We cannot understand Christ until we understand that He was the King of kings and the Lord of lords. Like Thomas, our only response must be to bow down and confess, "My Lord and my God!" (John 20:28).

December 21

GOD WITH US

Behold, the virgin shall conceive and bear a Son, and shall call His name Immanuel.
ISAIAH 7:14

I never come to Christmas without thinking of the thousands of people who are lonely and troubled at this time of year. I have had psychiatrists tell me their schedules are overloaded with people who find the Christmas season almost more than they can bear because of their loneliness and isolation.

Christmas is God's reminder that we are not alone. God revealed in the life, death, and resurrection of Jesus a reconciling love that rescues us from separation and loneliness. We are not alone; God has come down from Heaven to tell us He loves us!

At this Christmas season you can be assured that Jesus Christ is here. He is here to give us hope, to forgive our sins, to give us a new song, to impart faith, and to heal our spiritual wounds if only we will let Him.

The Christmas message has not changed after two thousand years. Christmas still reminds us that God is with us. If you are lonely this Christmas, welcome Christ into your life. Then ask Him to help you reach out to someone else who is lonely, and show that person His love.

HEAVENLY HERALD

*I have come that they may have life, and
that they may have it more abundantly.*
JOHN 10:10

Christmas is not just a date on the calendar. It is not just an annual holiday. It is not a day to glorify selfishness and materialism. Christmas is the celebration of the event that set Heaven to singing, an event that gave the stars of the night sky a new brilliance.

Christmas tells us that at a specific time and at a specific place a specific Person was born. That Person was (in the words of an ancient Christian creed) "God of God, Light of Light, very God of very God"—the Lord, Jesus Christ.

From the lips of Him who came fell these words: "The Son of Man has come to seek and to save that which was lost" (Luke 19:10). Like piercing trumpets, these words heralded the breaking in of the Divine to human history. They declare that Heaven has come to our rescue and that God has not left us to stumble alone on Earth's pathway. What a wonderful and glorious hope we have because of that first Christmas!

December 23

A HEALING WORD

I have called you friends.
JOHN 15:15

Christ came into a world that had problems much like the ones we grapple with today. Life was short, disease rampant, nations chafed under the heel of Roman rule, slavery was universal. Widows, orphans, the disabled and chronically ill had no social "safety net" to see them through the rough times.

To those without the joy of living, Jesus said, "I have come that they may have life, and that they may have it more abundantly" (John 10:10).

To those who bore the chafing burden of the guilt of sin, He said, "Be of good cheer; your sins are forgiven you" (Matt. 9:2).

To the friendless He said, "No longer do I call you servants . . . but I have called you friends" (John 15:15). He had a healing word for each one.

On the surface the world has changed radically since that first Christmas. But deep inside, our problems are the same—for they are problems of the heart. And Christ still comes to us to cleanse our guilt, give us hope for the future, and heal our hurts with His love.

LOOKING FOR PEACE

Glory to God in the highest, and on earth peace.
LUKE 2:14

The centuries have rolled by, and still the world longs for and looks for the peace the angels sang about on that first Christmas morning. Even the land of His birth often seems torn by violence and conflict. "Where is His peace?" you ask.

I'll tell you where it is. It abides in the hearts of all who have trusted His grace. And in the same proportion that the world has trusted in Christ, it also has peace. Yet our world continues to be torn by wars and unrest. I know of no country that is completely safe or completely at peace.

The greatest war of all, however, is the war between us and God, as we stubbornly rebel against His authority and defiantly seize control of our lives apart from Him. But now the war can be over, as we yield ourselves to Christ as our Lord. Then we have peace—peace with God, peace in our hearts, and peace with each other. Is the war over in your life?

December 25

ROOM FOR JESUS

She brought forth her firstborn Son,... and laid Him in a manger, because there was no room for them in the inn.
LUKE 2:7

No room for Jesus? No room for the King of kings? No, but room for others and for other things. There was no room for Jesus in the world that He had made—imagine!

Things have not really changed since that Bethlehem night over two thousand years ago. God is still on the fringes of most of our lives. We fit Him in when it is convenient for us, but we become irritated when He makes demands on us. If God would only stay in His little box and come out when we pull the string!

Our lives are so full. There is so much to be done. But in all our busy activities are we in danger of excluding from our hearts and lives the One who made us?

"Oh, come to my heart, Lord Jesus; there is room in my heart for you."

December 26

THE SUFFERING SERVANT

He was wounded for our transgressions.
ISAIAH 53:5

Jesus' life began in the midst of persecution and peril. He came on a mission of love and mercy, sent by the Father. An angel announced His conception and gave Him His name. The heavenly host sang a glorious anthem at His birth. By the extraordinary star, the very heavens indicated His coming. He was the most illustrious child ever born—the holy child of Mary, the divine Son of God.

Yet no sooner did He enter our world than Herod decreed His death and labored to accomplish it. Warned of God in a dream, Joseph fled Bethlehem at night, taking Mary and the baby Jesus to Egypt until Herod's death finally made it safe to return.

The Son of the eternal Father, He entered time and was made in the likeness of man. He assumed our human nature with all its infirmities, and weakness, and capacity for suffering. He came as a child of the poorest parents. His entire life was one long pathway of humiliation.

Now He is in Heaven, no longer limited by time and space. And someday He will come again—this time in glory—to take us to Himself.

December 27

GOD'S WISDOM

How unsearchable are His judgments
and His ways past finding out!
ROMANS 11:33

The end of another year is approaching, and people are already predicting what the new year holds. A year from now most of them probably will have missed the target!

The fact is, no one knows the future—except God. We even know so little about the world in which we live. No doubt scientists will continue to uncover astonishing facts about the universe. But even then, they will know only a miniscule amount compared with the total sum of potential knowledge.

But God is infinite! He knows it all—because He created it in the first place. We will always be bewildered and confused by what we don't know, if we are honest. We don't even know our immediate futures; as James said, "You do not know what will happen tomorrow" (James 4:14).

What should this mean? It should give us humility before God, and it should give us trust—trust in the God who does know our futures, and who works all things for His glory. You can trust all your tomorrows to Him!

December 28

Pass Along Comfort

Blessed be the God ... of all comfort.
2 Corinthians 1:3

A dear friend and trusted counselor once told me that sometimes the greatest test comes to us when we ask God the question, "Why?"

As Charles Hembree has pointed out, "In the full face of afflictions it is hard to see any sense to things that befall us, and we want to question the fairness of a faithful God. However, these moments can be the most meaningful of our lives."

Alexander Nowell once said, "God does not comfort us that we may be comforted but that we may be comforters." We are to pass along the comfort with which God has comforted us.

Look around you. There are countless opportunities to comfort others, not only in the loss of a loved one, but also in the daily distress that so often creeps into our lives. One of Paul's companions on some of his missionary journeys was named Joseph, "whom the apostles called Barnabas (which means Son of Encouragement)" (Acts 4:36, NIV). Will you be a Barnabas to someone today?

December 29

BRING GLORY TO GOD

Present . . . your members as
instruments of righteousness God.
ROMANS 6:13

When you serve sin, your body is dedicated to the service of sin. Your appetites, whetted by Satan, rage unthrottled. Your God-given creative impulses are sacrificed to Satan on the altar of lust. A sinner, in a sense, is a dedicated person, yielded to his appetites and selfish desires.

But when Christ comes into the human heart we are to yield our bodies to Him. Our human frame is often a rebellious and unruly servant. Only through rigid discipline and the help of the Holy Spirit are we able to master it into complete subjection to Christ. We must guard against appetites that blight the conscience, wither the soul, and weaken our witness for Christ.

Perhaps many things are lawful, but are they expedient? Are they a harmful example to others?

As long as we are in this world, our old nature will try to defeat us and turn us away from Christ. But learn to recognize the warning signs, and commit your mind and body to Christ "as instruments of righteousness."

December 30

GOD'S GIFTS TO US

We have different gifts, according to
the grace given to each of us.
ROMANS 12:6, NIV

If you are a parent you've undoubtedly had the experience of having your children complain after Christmas is over, disappointed they didn't get the gift they wanted or bored with the ones they received. It's not an easy problem to solve!

God our Father has given gifts to each of us, and I pray we may never become discontent or bored with them. The greatest gift of all, of course, is the gift of His Son. But the Bible also teaches God has given us other gifts—gifts that come from the Holy Spirit's ministry in our lives. These are the gifts of the Spirit, and they include everything from the gift of preaching to the gift of hospitality. None of us has every gift, but every Christian has at least one, to be used for one purpose: to build up Christ's body, the Church (Eph. 4:11–12).

What spiritual gift has God given you? Don't worry about those you don't have. Be content with those God has given you, and use them for His glory.

December 31

THE CITY OF GOD

There shall be no night there. . . .
And they shall reign forever and ever.
REVELATION 22:5

Many years ago I was visiting the dining room of the United States Senate. As I was speaking to various people, one of the senators said, "Billy, we're having a discussion about pessimism and optimism. Are you a pessimist or an optimist?" I smiled and said, "I'm an optimist." He asked, "Why?" I replied, "I've read the last page of the Bible."

The Bible speaks about a heavenly city whose builder and maker is God, where those who have been redeemed will be superior to angels. It speaks of "a pure river of water of life, clear as crystal, proceeding from the throne of God and of the Lamb" (Rev. 22:1). It says, "There shall be no night there: They need no lamp nor light of the sun, for the Lord God gives them light. And they shall reign forever and ever" (Rev. 22:5).

As another year ends, no doubt you have had your share of joys and disappointments. Don't live in the past, but "be patient and stand firm, because the Lord's coming is near" (James 5:8, NIV).

STEPS TO PEACE WITH GOD

1. RECOGNIZE GOD'S PLAN—PEACE AND LIFE

The message in this book stresses that
God loves you and wants you
to experience His peace and life.

The BIBLE says ... For God loved the
world so much that He gave His only Son,
so that everyone who believes in Him may
not die but have eternal life. John 3:16

2. REALIZE OUR PROBLEM—SEPARATION FROM GOD

People choose to disobey God and go
their own way. This results in
separation from God.

The BIBLE says ... Everyone has sinned
and is far away from God's saving
presence. Romans 3:23

3. RESPOND TO GOD'S REMEDY—THE CROSS OF CHRIST

God sent His Son to bridge the gap. Christ
did this by paying the penalty of our sins
when He died on the cross and rose from
the grave.

The BIBLE says ... But God has shown
us how much He loves us—it was while we
were still sinners that Christ died for us!
Romans 5:8

4. RECEIVE GOD'S SON—LORD AND SAVIOR

You cross the bridge into God's family
when you ask Christ to come into your life.

The BIBLE says ... Some, however, did
receive Him and believed in Him; so He
gave them the right to become God's
children. John 1:12

THE INVITATION IS TO:

REPENT (turn from your sins), ASK for God's forgiveness, and by faith RECEIVE
Jesus Christ into your heart and life and follow Him in obedience as your Lord
and Savior.

PRAYER OF COMMITMENT

"Dear Lord Jesus, I know that I am a sinner, and I ask for Your forgiveness. I believe
You died for my sins and rose from the dead. I turn from my sins and invite You to
come into my heart and life. I want to trust and follow You as my Lord and Savior.
In Your Name, amen."

If you are committing your life to Christ, please let us know!

Billy Graham Evangelistic Association
1 Billy Graham Parkway, Charlotte, NC 28201-0001
1-877-2GRAHAM (1-877-247-2426)
BillyGraham.org/Commitment